PUIR LABOURERS
AND
BUSY HUSBANDMEN

Fourteenth-century swing plough.

A swing plough, or heavy mould-board plough, depicted in the English Luttrell Psalter of the early fourteenth century. The swing plough used in Scotland had no wheel to support its front beam and had to be turned and steered entirely by the ploughman, unlike the wheeled plough used in some other parts of northern Europe.

Puir Labourers and Busy Husbandmen

The Countryside of Lowland Scotland in the Middle Ages

Piers Dixon

Series editor: Gordon Barclay

BIRLINN
with
HISTORIC SCOTLAND

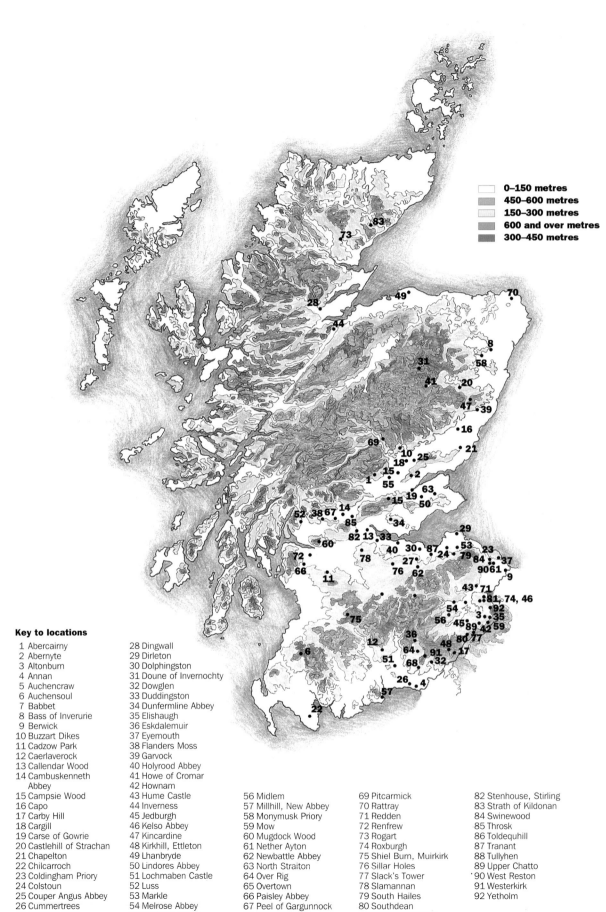

0–150 metres
450–600 metres
150–300 metres
600 and over metres
300–450 metres

Key to locations

1 Abercairny	28 Dingwall
2 Abernyte	29 Dirleton
3 Altonburn	30 Dolphingston
4 Annan	31 Doune of Invernochty
5 Auchencraw	32 Dowglen
6 Auchensoul	33 Duddingston
7 Babbet	34 Dunfermline Abbey
8 Bass of Inverurie	35 Elishaugh
9 Berwick	36 Eskdalemuir
10 Buzzart Dikes	37 Eyemouth
11 Cadzow Park	38 Flanders Moss
12 Caerlaverock	39 Garvock
13 Callendar Wood	40 Holyrood Abbey
14 Cambuskenneth	41 Howe of Cromar
Abbey	42 Hownam
15 Campsie Wood	43 Hume Castle
16 Capo	44 Inverness
17 Carby Hill	45 Jedburgh
18 Cargill	46 Kelso Abbey
19 Carse of Gowrie	47 Kincardine
20 Castlehill of Strachan	48 Kirkhill, Ettleton
21 Chapelton	49 Lhanbryde
22 Chilcarroch	50 Lindores Abbey
23 Coldingham Priory	51 Lochmaben Castle
24 Colstoun	52 Luss
25 Couper Angus Abbey	53 Markle
26 Cummertrees	54 Melrose Abbey
27 Dalkeith Park	55 Methven Wood

56 Midlem	69 Pitcarmick	82 Stenhouse, Stirling
57 Millhill, New Abbey	70 Rattray	83 Strath of Kildonan
58 Monymusk Priory	71 Redden	84 Swinewood
59 Mow	72 Renfrew	85 Throsk
60 Mugdock Wood	73 Rogart	86 Toldequhill
61 Nether Ayton	74 Roxburgh	87 Tranant
62 Newbattle Abbey	75 Shiel Burn, Muirkirk	88 Tullyhen
63 North Straiton	76 Sillar Holes	89 Upper Chatto
64 Over Rig	77 Slack's Tower	90 West Reston
65 Overtown	78 Slamannan	91 Westerkirk
66 Paisley Abbey	79 South Hailes	92 Yetholm
67 Peel of Gargunnock	80 Southdean	
68 Pennersaughs	81 Springwood Park	

Contents

Broad rig.

Aerial photograph of the high-backed broad ridge and furrow still preserved in the golf course of Prestonfield Golf Course. Rig of this type was a typical feature of the medieval countryside. While it is not certain if it was first introduced by the Anglo-Normans, it probably spread to most of lowland Scotland during the medieval period.

CROWN COPYRIGHT RCAHMS

Introduction

'Esope, mine author makis mention
Of twa myis, and they were sisteris dear,
Of wham the eldest dwelt in ane boroughis toun
The other wynnit upon land weill neir'...
This rural mouse, into the wynter tyde,
Had hunger, cauld, and tholit great distress.
The other mouse, that in the borough can byde, ...
Toll free als, but custom mair or less,
And freedom had to ga whair ever she list.'

The Taill of the Uplandis Mous and Burges Mous,
Robert Henryson, *c*.1425–*c*.1506.

As Henryson revealed in his rendering of the
Aesop fable, the differences between town and
country life were already evident in the fifteenth
century. Our understanding of rural life in medieval
Scotland has been hampered by the lack of any
obvious points of reference beyond the castles and
abbeys. Unlike midland England there are few
deserted medieval villages in the central belt of
Scotland, because of the efficiency with which
agricultural improvers swept away the old 'touns'
of post-medieval Scotland – the cleared townships
of the Highlands reflect relatively recent history.
As a result, archaeologists have been slow to get to
grips with the lowland medieval landscape. To date,
its description has been the field of documentary
historians and historical geographers and the
evidence has to be teased out.

In the thirteenth century the lowland countryside
of Scotland had many features that would have been
familiar to a traveller from England or northern
Europe. Much of the south and east from Berwick
to Inverness was 'champagne' country – open fields,
few enclosures and small village settlements or *touns*.
There was apparently none of the 'bocage', or
wooded landscape of small, hedged fields, with its
continuity from the medieval period, which has
been called 'ancient countryside' in England. This is
not to say that there were no enclosures in Scotland.
Hedges and enclosures are documented, and there
are some pre-Improvement field enclosures, but

they are probably post-medieval. The Scottish
landscape was essentially cleared of its tree cover in
later prehistory, so that what woodland remained
was limited in its distribution. How it was managed
has become the focus of a renewed interest in
woodland history.

This book explores these areas under three main
headings: housing and settlements, land use and rural
industry. The book focuses on the medieval period,

Motte.
Aerial photograph of the motte at Doune of Invernochty,
Aberdeenshire. Mottes are the characteristic defensive site introduced
by the Anglo-Normans in the twelfth and thirteenth centuries. This is
an example of a natural mound sculpted to form a motte, built for the
Earl of Mar.
CROWN COPYRIGHT RCAHMS

but the seventeenth and eighteenth centuries are discussed where relevant. But first we need to consider economic and social changes through the medieval period.

The Transformation of the Countryside in the Twelfth and Thirteenth Centuries

The countryside of lowland Scotland was transformed in the course of the twelfth and thirteenth centuries. An influx of Anglo-Norman and Flemish immigrants, many of whom were followers of King David I from his time in England as Earl of Huntingdon, brought Scotland into the mainstream of western Christendom. A 'feudal' system of landholding was gradually introduced and with it, many characteristics typical of northern Europe. Burghs were established by the king in order to manage trade, new feudal estates were created which the incomers held in return for military service, and reformed monasteries were

founded for the greater glory of God. The feudal estate was focused upon a new type of estate centre, the earthwork castle, or motte, such as the Bass of Inverurie in the Garioch, Aberdeenshire. The new monasteries such as Melrose and Kelso attracted grants of land with which to support the contemplative life and to build the magnificent conventual buildings we see today. These incomers brought with them new technologies and management methods already common in England and northern Europe. In addition, King David enforced the taking of tithes (*teinds* in Scots) for the support of the parochial church, which led to the construction of many new parish churches. The new landowners also founded feudal villages, whose inhabitants supplied the burgh markets, the supermarkets of their day. Alongside these innovations, Anglo-French styles of hunt

Planned village.
Midlem Village, Roxburghshire, from the air. This village encapsulates the classic features of the medieval planned village with its arrangement of properties and houses in rows around a green or street in common ownership. The Anglo-Normans established many such villages in the twelfth and thriteenth centuries.
CROWN COPYRIGHT RCAHMS

management were brought to Scotland, as extensive forest reserves were created (see map). Within the forest, land use was as controlled as in a National Nature Reserve of today, with the main interest being the maintenance of the deer stock and its habitat for hunting by the king or his barons.

Many of the rural characteristics of northern Europe came to be identifiable in the lowland parts of Scotland. These included the *demesne* or home farm, the village inhabited by serfs performing labour services on the demesne such as harvesting and the carriage of goods, strip fields, later known as *runrig*, the heavy mould-board plough and broad

ridge cultivation, and the estate grain mill. There was a simultaneous growth in industrial activity, much of it rurally based, including the manufacture of earthenware pottery, the extraction of iron, mostly bog iron, to make tools in the estate forge, the development of water power, usually for milling grain, and the mining of silver and lead.

It would be wrong, however, to assume that there were no trends in this direction before the twelfth century. In south-east Scotland, for example, and in Berwickshire in particular, the charters of King Edgar indicate that many of the settlement units or townships were already established by the late eleventh century. Equally, twelfth-century charters refer to many of the fields in these townships by Anglo-Scandinavian names, which suggests that the fields must have developed after the influx of Scandinavians in the tenth century. This may have a bearing on the date at which strip fields, the heavy mould-board plough and broad ridge cultivation were introduced into Scotland (see page 31ff).

The kingdom of Scotland in the twelfth century comprised an ethnic mix: Anglo-Scandinavians of Northumbria in the south-east, Gaelic speakers and Scandinavians in the south-west, Britons in Strathclyde, and Picts north of the Forth with a veneer of Gaelic-speaking Scots, who also dominated the south-west Highlands of Argyll. This led to a variation in rural practices throughout Scotland, as suggested by the terminology of land assessment in the different areas. In the central belt and south-east, the *ploughgate* (the land cultivable by a plough drawn by an eight-oxen team in one year: about 104 acres) was used as a unit of measurement,

Mountainous regions

Forest first recorded between 1124–1200

Forest first recorded between 1200–1286

Map of hunting reserves.
Map of hunting reserves or forests in Scotland, both royal and baronial. As may be seen, large parts of lowland Scotland were incorporated into them.
AFTER ATLAS OF SCOTTISH HISTORY

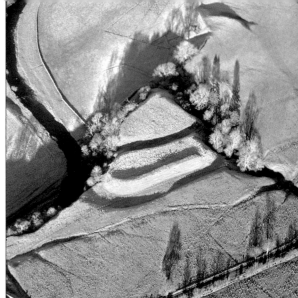

(above left)
Monastic precinct.
Aerial photograph of Crossraguel Abbey showing the cloisters and outer court of the Cluniac monastery.
CROWN COPYRIGHT RCAHMS

(above right)
Earthwork castle.
The earthwork at Castleton is the site of Liddel Castle, seat of the de Soulis lords of Liddesdale. The castle was formed by cutting off a promontory jutting out into the flood plain of the River Liddel and was replaced by Hermitage Castle during the Scots Wars of Independence.
CROWN COPYRIGHT RCAHMS

while in the Pictish realms north of the Forth and the south-west the *davoch* (the amount of land that produces a standard vat of grain in tax) was used.

The available archaeological evidence points to a significant change in settlement in the twelfth century. The population and economy were expanding with the result that many new medieval settlements were founded. There is documentation for the founding of new settlements by incomers, for example, in one Lothian township, the *villa* (village) of Doddin (later Duddingston) replaced the Celtic Treverlen in the twelfth century. The influx of a new Anglo-Norman aristocracy, and of so many other northern Europeans in their wake, ensured that a new uniformity for the management of estates and the produce of the countryside was established. By the later thirteenth century, we find that many of the tenantry of lowland Scotland were using Anglo-French names, and the 'native' landowners such as the Earls of Mar and Fife were indistinguishable from their Anglo-Norman peers.

Late Medieval Economic and Social Change

It is against this background that the Scottish Wars of Independence took place, leading to much disruption of the countryside, with repeated invasions and devastations throughout the fourteenth century, particularly in the south and east, where the English occupation lasted longest and was most hotly contested. Some areas such as the forest of Ettrick passed to and fro between English and Scottish control, while Annandale centred around the castle of Lochmaben was largely in English hands for half of the fourteenth century. Indeed, following the English occupation, the major southern Scottish trading centres of Berwick and Roxburgh never recovered their pre-war position of importance. Roxburgh failed altogether and was abandoned after 1460 and Berwick became an English bastion from 1482. It is difficult to demonstrate the direct effects of warfare upon

Assart

In a hunting forest, the enclosure of land for agriculture and settlement, called an assart, was licensed, and had to be surrounded by a ditch and hedge. Here a cruck-framed house is being built. Charcoal-burning is in progress in the foreground.
DAVID SIMON

Parish church.

This Romanesque church of St Cuthbert at Dalmeny in West Lothian typifies the simple cellular structure found at so many parish churches, having a west tower, an aisleless nave and presbytery. The tower here is a modern replacement. This is one of the most complete twelfth-century examples in Scotland.
CROWN COPYRIGHT RCAHMS

individual settlements archaeologically, but contemporary documentary accounts report severe devastation in many parts of southern Scotland.

Added to this traumatic picture were successive major outbreaks of plague in 1349–50 and 1362. Described by John of Fordun, the fourteenth-century chronicler, as being responsible for carrying off nearly a third of the population, particularly 'the meaner sort', they led to a drastic change in the medieval economy with an accompanying social change at the end of the fourteenth century. The general economic effects were significant. The temporary, but severe, devastation of warfare, combined with the Black Death, made it difficult for landlords to find tenants. Indeed, from the later fourteenth century, even the Crown found it difficult to find tenants and touns are often stated to be vacant. Rents fell as landlords strove to keep their tenants on the land; labour costs rose and home farms (demesnes) were leased to farmers, as landlords, lay and ecclesiastical, found it easier to collect rent than to hire expensive labour. Serfdom,

already on the decline, disappeared altogether to be replaced by the husbandman, the pre-eminent style of tenant farmer of the late medieval period, and the cottar or smallholder. The husbandman, 'honest yeman', held between one and four *oxgangs* (one oxgang comprises 13 acres of arable) and could take advantage of the cheap rents. There may have been a retreat from the cultivation of marginal land as settlements and arable land were abandoned.

Perhaps in reaction to the trauma of the fourteenth century the late medieval period saw a change in settlement pattern as touns were replaced by a dispersed pattern of smaller touns and farms. The evidence for this has to be teased out from what appear to be divergent trends in the fifteenth century. At the same time as there are repeated records of vacant touns and steadings in the Crown rentals, the splitting of townships is an indication of a renewed growth in population and the economy. Furthermore, there was increasing pressure on land in the royal forests, such as Alyth and Clunie in Perthshire, with new farms being settled. The possibility remains that a renewed expansion of settlement in the late medieval period has obscured the evidence of an earlier retreat, with the same sites being resettled. Meanwhile, particularly in lowland areas, former touns were replaced by new settlements. In the Cupar Angus Abbey estates, for example, touns were subdivided, and in the Borders, village settlements such as Swinewood and Nether Ayton in Coldinghamshire disappeared to be replaced by a rash of new farms.

It is against this background that the desertion of the settlements at Springwood, Kelso and Rattray, Aberdeenshire (described below), in the fourteenth and fifteenth centuries respectively should be viewed. These were hardly marginal settlements in the normal sense of the word, but village settlements in relatively rich arable land. Springwood, for example, may have been deserted because of one of a number of disasters typifying the fourteenth century such as plague or warfare, the temporary lack of tenants being followed by resettlement in a different location. This process of desertion, accompanied by the splitting of touns, provided a background for a change in the pattern of settlement from one dominated by villages to a more dispersed pattern. In addition to the splitting of touns, some new farms are documented, perhaps the result of the creation of *feu* tenancies giving security of tenure. These were popular from about 1500, particularly on monastic and Crown estates, such as the forest of Ettrick. Another late-medieval trend was towards larger and longer tenancies, and the so-called *kindly* tenures whereby tenants were allowed to continue in occupation year-on-year at the discretion of the landowner. In such circumstances tenants were better able to sustain the requirements of defence and also to invest in the fortified houses that proliferated in southern Scotland in the late sixteenth century (e.g. Slacks Tower, Roxburghshire).

The medieval countryside created in the twelfth to fourteenth century was not static. What is significant is that the unenclosed landscape of rig that John Slezer depicted in his topographical views of the principal towns and houses in 1693 was to be swept away by the improvements of the eighteenth and nineteenth centuries. It is a countryside that is foreign to us, and one which the improvements of the Agricultural Revolution replaced with the familiar one of enclosed rectilinear fields defined by hedge, stone dyke, or wire fence.

Fortified farmhouse.
During the late sixteenth and early seventeenth centuries a rash of houses were built in southern Scotland by lesser gentry or lairds. These aped the tower houses of their social superiors, but were essentially glorified farmhouses. They were called a variety of things including bastle houses and pele houses to indicate their defensive features. Slack's Tower belies its name, but exemplifies the type.
CROWN COPYRIGHT RCAHMS

Rigged fields, Slezer 1693.
An example of a pre-Improvement agricultural landscape at Scone by John Slezer 1693, showing the village of Scone and the extensive rigged land that would have typified lowland Scotland before the Improvements. *The Prospect of the House and Town of Scone*, 1693.
CROWN COPYRIGHT RCAHMS

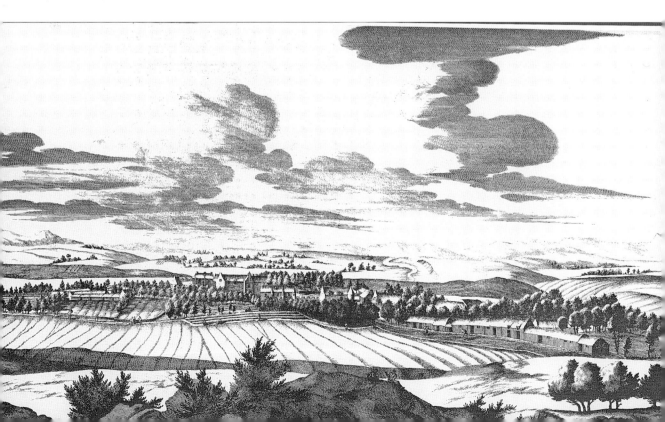

Housing and Settlements

'Puir laboureris and busy husbandmen
Went wet and weary draglit in the fen;
The silly sheep and their little herd-groomis
Lurkis under lea of bankis, wodis, and broomis;
And other dantit greater bestial,
Within their stabillis sesyt into stall,
Sic as mulis, horsis, oxen and kye,
Fed tuskit boaris, and fat swine in sty,
Sustainit were by manis governance
On harvest and simmeris purveyance.'

Winter, Gavin Douglas, *c.*1474–1522

The Pre-Improvement Settlement Landscape

Little now remains to remind us of Scotland's rural landscape as it was before the great transformation of the Agricultural Revolution (about 1750 to 1850). General Roy's map of Scotland, compiled in the aftermath of Bonnie Prince Charlie's ill-fated campaign of 1745–46, provides a glimpse of it. The landscape it reveals is one of a few small urban settlements and many small irregular groups of buildings that would have been called 'touns' in Old Scots. There were few enclosed fields that we would recognise today, and those that did exist were recent creations.

Roy mapped most arable land diagrammatically, using patches of parallel lines to depict strip fields. His map was at a scale of one inch to the mile and the picture, like a modern 1:50,000 map, was very generalised. However, it provides a good starting point and is without parallel in earlier periods. Pont, the first surveyor to map rural settlements in Scotland, made sketches in the 1590s that later formed the basis for Blaeu's Atlas of 1654, but these were at an even smaller scale. Fortunately, many estate maps were drawn up for landowners in the 1760s and 1770s in the early phase of the Agricultural Revolution. These provide the best and most detailed view of the farming landscape before the improved farms were laid out. The small rural 'touns' shown on these plans are much more varied than they appear from Roy. In the lowland areas of the south and east there are examples of small row or street 'villages' such as West Reston in Berwickshire or Overtown and Abernyte in Perthshire, while others, such as Cargill in Perthshire, are actually the irregular agglomerations suggested by General Roy. What the estate maps also show us are the irregular 'blobs' of the fields around the settlements, often shaded or

(opposite, above)
Roy's map.
An extract from General Roy's map of Scotland (1747-55) of the Huntly area, showing the unenclosed rural landscape of the mid-eighteenth century.
BRITISH LIBRARY

(opposite, below)
Sixteenth-century village plan.
A spy map of Eyemouth Fort and Village in 1560, showing two rows of houses on either side of a street. The alignment matches that of the modern High Street.
BRITISH LIBRARY

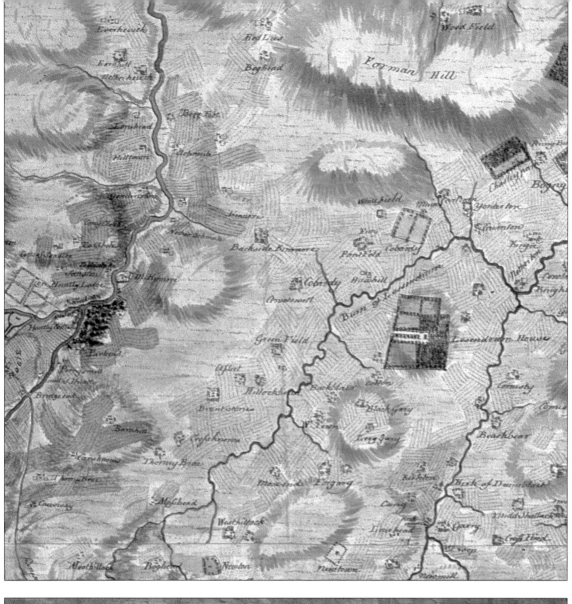

Eighteenth-century village plan.
An eighteenth-century estate plan of Abernyte and Overtown villages showing the rows of houses and house-plots typical of a lowland row village.
NATIONAL LIBRARY OF SCOTLAND

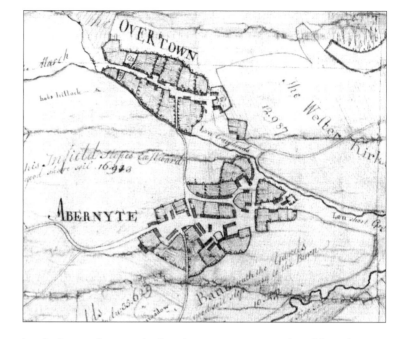

Rattray manor.
Rattray manor, Aberdeenshire, during excavation, showing the foundations of the fourteenth-century manorial buildings that stood on the twelfth-century motte.
CROWN COPYRIGHT HISTORIC SCOTLAND

hatched according to whether they were permanently cultivated infield or occasionally cultivated outfield. Sometimes, but more rarely, they show the curving strips of runrig, where more than one proprietor was involved. Because of the late date of these surveys, it is open to debate as to how representative they are of the medieval rural landscape. We cannot presume that farming was static over a period of 500 years.

Contemporary Evidence for Settlement

There are no contemporary paintings or drawings of medieval rural settlement; indeed, there are no images of rural settlements in Scotland before the sixteenth century. The earliest images are those illustrating the *Scotichronicon*, a fifteenth-century chronicle of the kingdom of Scotland by Walter Bower, but these show towns, for example, the illustration of the siege of Stirling. A few drawings of settlements are to be found in maps made by English spies: one of Eyemouth village in Berwickshire dating to about 1560 shows the French artillery fort and the village as a single street with houses on either side. Similarly, a sketch of part of Annandale of the same date shows the defences and houses of the burgh of Annan. Both, however, are somewhat scant and little can be said about the houses, but comparison with the modern alignment of the high streets of both settlements suggests that the sixteenth-century high streets are on the same line as today. Since one settlement was a fishing village and the other a burgh, neither is wholly typical of the wider rural scene.

Contemporary descriptions of settlement are equally rare. Blind

Shieling hut.
A turf-walled shieling-hut from Glen Nochty, Aberdeenshire.

Harry's *Wallace* dating to the 1470s describes a siege by Wallace of the Peel of Gargunnock, Stirlingshire, which gives an image of a ditched enclosure, entered by a drawbridge, and containing a hall, chamber and courtyard. This conjures up a moated manor, like the manorial sites recently excavated at Rattray, Aberdeenshire, or the group of buildings at the thirteenth-century Caerlaverock Castle, Dumfriesshire. However, poetic imagery tells us little of the architecture or layout of the buildings themselves.

Records of property disputes shed the most useful light on rural settlement. A complaint of 1559, for example, concerning the destruction of certain huts called *schelis* made of *faill and dovett* (thick and thin turves for use in the walls and roof respectively) at a shieling called Toldequhill in Strathdon, Aberdeenshire, reminds us of the use of perishable materials in the construction of summer shelters. Such early allusions to building materials are, however, rare.

Most contemporary medieval records were written for legal transactions of property, such as charters, or for taxation or accounting: few accounts are mere description. Such charters may detail the layout of the property, but the associated rights such as grazing, or access to wood are often generalised. Charters are most frequently preserved in the monastic cartularies (collected copies of charters written into one book) and provide a key source of information for the period from 1150 to 1550.

The cartularies also occasionally include copies of surveys of the monastic estates. The earliest known are from about 1300 for the monasteries of Kelso and Coldingham; they provide a snapshot of the monastic properties at that time. Unfortunately, the only equivalent survey for a lay estate is that of the earldom of Fife of 1294–95, when in royal hands. There is then nothing extensive until 1376, when there is a rental record of the Douglas of Dalkeith estates in southern Scotland, including lands in Fife, Peeblesshire, Eskdale and Liddesdale. As a result, our knowledge of rural settlement in the twelfth and thirteenth centuries is biased towards the monastic estate. Rental records remain patchy in their coverage until the later seventeenth century, when surviving estate rentals become more common.

Details of settlement are therefore hard to find; we depend upon the occasional shafts of light shed by royal grants of property (e.g. in the Register of the Great Seal), or in the accounts of royal lands submitted to the treasury in the Exchequer Rolls. Our picture therefore has to be built from the details in the documents that survive, and from archaeology, and there is always a danger that 'common-sense' assumptions are merely modern preconceived notions.

The picture that does emerge from our limited sources is of varied communities. Settlements are described in different terms – *tenementum,* or holding (which is not very explicit and could be a whole township or a much smaller plot in a village), *villa* or village (although this was often used to denote both the village and the lands of the inhabitants) *terra,* literally a piece of land (which could be a

Monastic grange.

The site of Colpenhope Grange, belonging to Kelso Abbey, in the Halterburn Valley of the Cheviots, is marked by a ditched square enclosure. This grange was mainly involved in sheep and cattle farming.

P. J. DIXON

township or farm) and *grangia* or grange (usually a farm separate from the abbey run exclusively by Cistercian monks). Of these, the odd one out is the grange since this is the closest to a modern farm, in that it was a single unit with a discrete piece of land to cultivate. The context in which the above terms are used is significant, and we cannot assume that each term has only one meaning.

Individual holdings are described in documents as *capital messuage*, or manor house of the feudal lord, which may include a home farm; the *husbandland* or tenant farm, based on the *messuage* or *toft* (where the house is to be found), and the *cotagia* or smallholding, which may have an acre or two of land and a cottage. Labourers, who did most of the work, do not even figure in the documents, yet they must have lived somewhere. All the types of settlement noted above may be found in a single village and are described as such in the surveys and charters.

The layout of villages is suggested by the descriptions in medieval charters. Some charters specify the location of a messuage or a toft next to another or between others or even occasionally in a row of tofts. A charter of Coldingham Priory dated 1275, for example, records the grant of:

> a messuage with buildings in the east part of the village [villa] of Auchencraw between the house of the lord Robert of Blakburn on the one side and lord David of Paxton on the other and 20 acres of arable and meadow in the territory of the same village [villa].

Another charter of 1326 describes the grant:

> by Adam son of Thomas de Capellam of one steading [messuage] lying between the toft of Roger Gudesband on the west side and the toft of the Prior of Coldingham in West Reston on the east.

Other charters differentiate between lands in the territory, or the fields of the village, and tofts in the village of the same name. The cumulative evidence from the charters for settlement in the lowland areas of south and east Scotland is for villages comprising rows of houses.

Archaeological Field Remains

Surviving remains of abandoned medieval settlements may be found in rough pasture, where they have not been removed by later farming; more rarely, they appear as cropmarks in arable fields, or as scatters of medieval artefacts in the ploughsoil. Most sites in pasture are located on the margins of modern farmland and survive for that reason. Only a handful of medieval sites have been located in ploughed farmland from scatters of medieval pottery, and most of these lie in south and

The striped cropmarks in the fields near Leuchars, Fife, are produced by infill of the furrows of levelled broad rig; here as much as 15 to 20 metres in width from furrow to furrow.

CROWN COPYRIGHT RCAHMS

Early medieval byre house.

Excavations in progress at the early medieval settlement at Pitcarmick in Perthshire. Note the byre marked by the line of flat stones, flanked by the low earthen banks of the collapsed turf or wattle and daub walls of the house.

CROWN COPYRIGHT RCAHMS

east Scotland as far north as Fife. Yet it is often the settlements in this type of land that are best documented in the medieval period. This presents us with a dichotomy in the evidence. There are archaeological sites in the rough pastures with no medieval documentation and documented sites in arable farmland with little obvious archaeology. So to what extent can any sort of picture be drawn from this unpromising distribution of evidence?

What survives is the key question, since we can only work with what has escaped the changes of recent centuries. What has survived depends upon the patterns of land use since the Agricultural Revolution. Some standing buildings survive that use traditional methods of construction and help elucidate how medieval houses may have been built. However, there are few obvious features from the medieval centuries for us to contemplate. Indeed, in the arable fields of modern farms, aerial photography is the best tool to discover the traces of human impact on the landscape showing as crop or soilmarks. The most obvious and visible features are the marks of former strip cultivation – these are frequently to be seen because of the deep marks left by the plough furrows. However, of settlement and houses little can be made out because of the construction methods that were employed. It has been observed in jest that the archaeology of the medieval period is all in the topsoil, but there is some truth in this. Cropmarks tend to be created by the presence of pits and ditches in the subsoil, but most medieval buildings were not constructed with foundations, therefore there is little possibility of them creating cropmarks.

There are also problems identifying sites in permanent pasture. The archaeologist is confronted with the overgrown remains of settlements that were often abandoned before the advent of detailed mapping began in the 1850s. Until the mid-1st millennium AD, most houses appear to have been round. After that time they tend to have been more or less rectangular, and medieval and later buildings are distinguished by their shape. However, until quite recently, archaeological excavations of rectangular buildings have dated them to the seventeenth and eighteenth centuries, and medieval buildings have been hard to find.

Early medieval settlements

Since the 1980s there has been great success in locating sites that can be dated to the earlier part of the medieval period. In upland areas of Perthshire long buildings have been recognised: 10–30 metres long by 7–8.5 metres broad, with walls of turf or turf and stone, they have rounded ends, bowed sides, and often an oblong hollow in one part of the interior. Their size and shape distinguish them from other, later medieval buildings. Most have been located singly or in small clusters of two or three in rough pasture or on moorland.

Excavation of two of these buildings at Pitcarmick in Perthshire has shown that the walls were largely built of turf. They had rounded stone-based end walls and an entrance offset in one of the long sides. They were divided into two compartments, a smaller domestic area with a hearth and a larger byre end, defined by a central soakaway, suggesting that we have here an early form of longhouse, designed to house both humans and animals. The hearth of the larger house produced three radiocarbon dates ranging from AD 600 to AD 895 and the hearth of the smaller a single date of AD 897 to AD 1012. At this stage, with only one site excavated, the dating of this phase of expansion into the marginal upland must be viewed as early medieval or Pictish rather than high medieval. Outside Perthshire, few early medieval buildings of this type have been located.

Medieval and post-medieval settlements

The earthworks of other types of long rectangular buildings have been located in many parts of the upland margins of southern Scotland that may turn out to have been occupied in the high medieval period. However, as little or no excavation has been carried out, the dating of these sites must remain uncertain.

Circumstantial documentary evidence suggests that these upland settlements in southern Scotland were well-established by the fourteenth century and could have been abandoned at any time from then until the eighteenth century. Possible reasons for desertion range

Turf-walled buildings.
Aerial photograph of a farmstead on Kirkhill, Liddesdale. The buildings were constructed with turf walls, and there are at least three different periods of house visible here. The farmstead was the focus of a medieval intake or assart defined by a bank and external ditch that is visible running diagonally across the photograph.
CROWN COPYRIGHT RCAHMS

Medieval farmstead.
A farmstead at Southean in the forest of Jedburgh, abandoned sometime before 1541. It comprises a main building (A) and two subsidiary buildings and an enclosure.
CROWN COPYRIGHT RCAHMS

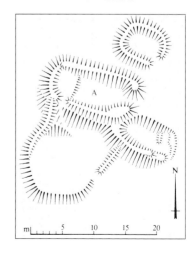

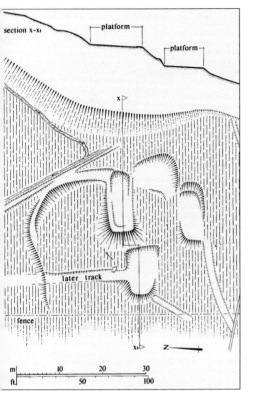

from the Black Death and the devastations of the Scottish Wars of Independence to the amalgamation of farms and the conversion of arable to pasture. Therefore, at least some of these sites may be medieval rather than later. In Southdean, near Jedburgh, several farmsteads were probably abandoned in the 1400s, since they are not recorded in a Crown rental of 1541. This abandonment took place before the clearance of farms that occurred in the 1700s, when landowners found it paid better to run sheep on the land rather than let farms to tenants, and arable land was turned to pasture. In Liddesdale there is documentary evidence that about one-quarter of the farmsteads were empty in 1541, and for the disappearance of others from the records in the early 1600s as farms were amalgamated. A similar phase of farm desertion occurred in neighbouring Wauchopdale and Eskdale in Dumfriesshire in the course of the 1600s, as tenants migrated to Ulster.

(left)
Platformed houses.
Plan of the farmstead at Effgillgate in Eskdale, Dumfriesshire. This type of platformed house is typical of the upland dales of southern Scotland in the medieval period.
CROWN COPYRIGHT RCAHMS

(below)
Deserted village.
The deserted village of Upper Chatto comprises a street with the site of houses on either side that is visible in front of the modern steading. A moated manor lay by the trees on the other side of the burn from the village.
M. RITCHIE

These settlements were farmsteads, typifying upland-edge settlement; they took the form of a main building about 10–20 metres long and 4–6 metres across, with an adjacent enclosure and perhaps some additional small buildings. Many of the buildings have been described as platform-buildings because of the way they are set into the slope. The walls are of stone or turf. Some of the buildings were longhouses, with the evidence of a byre-drain in one end suggesting that humans and cattle occupied different ends of the same building.

In the lowlands, archaeologists have recognised the remains of village settlements. At Hume Castle in Berwickshire and Upper Chatto in Roxburghshire, there are the earthworks of villages, comprising rows of houses and enclosures arranged along a street. At other sites such as Nether Ayton in Berwickshire, or Markle in East Lothian, fragmentary features such as track ways alone survive to suggest the location of deserted villages. As with the upland settlements, close dating of village establishment and abandonment is not possible, and little excavation has taken place. Documentation suggests that the lowland settlements date back to the twelfth century, if not earlier, and that some like Hume Castle were cleared in the course of the Agricultural Revolution, but others like Nether Ayton suffered a late medieval decline.

We can gain a good impression of what a medieval village looked like from the modern villages of Midlem, Roxburghshire, or Dirleton, East Lothian, which preserve the medieval arrangement of rows of houses and properties facing on to a street or green.

Planned village and castle.
Dirleton village and thirteenth-century castle, East Lothian. The village, like Midlem, displays a plan made up of rows of properties and houses arranged around an open space or green. The castle appears to be imposed on the south side of the village, which suggests a pre-thirteenth-century origin for the village layout.
CROWN COPYRIGHT RCAHMS

The survival of traditional buildings

There are several reasons why medieval sites are more difficult to find than post-medieval sites. First, perishable materials such as clay, turf and timber were used in house construction; second, medieval houses lacked foundations.

In areas such as the Carse of Gowrie in Perthshire or lowland Dumfriesshire, it is still possible to find traditional houses with clay walls. The roofs of these houses were often supported on cruck-trusses, comprising pairs of timbers arranged in an A-frame, bonded by a collar at the top and a lower collar beam above head height. Ridge-beams and purlins joined the trusses and provided the

Cruck house.
Interior of a cruck-framed cottage at Torthorwald in Dumfriesshire.
CROWN COPYRIGHT RCAHMS

support for the rafters (cabers), on which the roof covering of turf and thatch or heather and thatch was laid. Many such roofs may survive hidden beneath corrugated iron erected in the twentieth century. The remains of turf-walled buildings are less well-preserved, because by their nature the decay of the organic element makes the walls unstable. There are nineteenth-century photographs of interleaved turf and stone shielings and we know from eighteenth- and nineteenth- century descriptions that both turf or interleaved turf and stone were techniques used to construct walls for buildings in parts of southern Scotland. Walls were also built of wattles (*stake and rice* – posts woven with flexible twigs) which were then covered by clay (*daub*); again little archaeological trace might survive.

Access to suitable building materials was a key factor in the selection of a method of construction, hence the use of clay, turf or wattle. However, despite the use of perishable materials, the walls of the buildings were often based upon stone to make a dry foundation for the turf or clay superstructure, and the foot of the crucks. In addition, the use of cruck-trusses, widespread in pre-nineteenth- century Scottish housing, means that the walls of most rural houses were not designed to be load-bearing, but as an infilling to keep out the weather. There is no need for foundations in a building of this kind, and it is usually the survival of the footings that identifies the site.

Cruck Barn.

The cruck barn at Prior's Linn, Canonbie, Dumfriesshire, has a roof carried on cruck trusses, which are found on stone plinths in a clay wall. It typifies the type of barn that would have been common before the agricultural improvements where suitable clay for building was to be found.

CROWN COPYRIGHT RCAHMS

Archaeological Excavations

Only two excavations since the mid-1980s have revealed traces of rural buildings of the twelfth to fifteenth centuries: Springwood Park near Kelso in the Borders and Rattray in Aberdeenshire. A third site which probably also dates to before the end of the 1600s is Dowglen in Eskdale.

Lowland villages

At Springwood the buildings were arranged in a single row, fronting a natural terrace, 150 metres south of the modern Teviot Bridge. The medieval potsherds in the ploughsoil that led to the original identification of the site were also found in the area between the terrace and the bridge, suggesting the settlement extended as far as the bridge. Ditches seem to have been used to define plots of land, although at Springwood this does not appear to have continued throughout the whole history of the settlement; however, there is clear evidence that two major reorganisations of the settlement took place in the thirteenth and fourteenth centuries. On both occasions the alignment of the buildings was turned through a right-angle from face-on to the terrace to end-on and back again.

When excavated, the fourteenth-century houses at Springwood looked as if they were stone-walled; what was visible was not the bottom of load-bearing walls, but only wall foundations. The roofs of the buildings were supported on crucks. The walls were generally 70–90 centimetres thick and up to about 40 centimetres high (two courses of stonework). The core was packed with earth and stone and where the facings had been subsequently removed for use elsewhere, this core was sometimes the only thing that remained. Spread alongside the walls in one of the buildings was a layer of small stones interleaved with silt. It seems likely that this is the remnant of a collapsed clay wall, which was built on top of the footing; the small stones would have been a filler or aggregate, sometimes called clay-boule.

About one-third of the way along the back wall of one of the fourteenth-century buildings was a broken flat slab set in the wall footing about 0.5 metres above the floor. This fortuitous survival initiated a search for other cruck-settings and several were located in the earlier thirteenth-century phase of buildings. These earlier houses were also based on a low stone footing. However, in this period of occupation several variants on a cruck-setting, were encountered,

Excavated fourteenth-century houses.
Excavations at Springwood Park, Kelso, showing the row of fourteenth-century buildings. Note the cobbled stand at the end of the houses more probably for stalling horses than cows.
P.J. DIXON

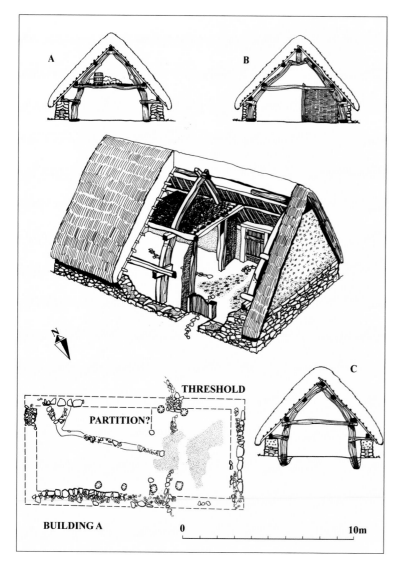

Options for reconstructing the cruck houses at Springwood Park, Kelso, in the thirteenth and fourteenth centuries. The variety of cruck-foundations and wall-infills are shown.
CROWN COPYRIGHT HISTORIC SCOTLAND

THRESHOLD

PARTITION?

BUILDING A

0   10m

including one that was set in a post-hole and had undergone a major resetting, another that was set in a shallow post-hole in the corner of one of the buildings, and a third that was set on a flat pad-stone laid on the ground.

The interiors of thirteenth- and fourteenth-century houses at Springwood have certain common features. They were all 8–13 metres long by 3.5–4.5 metres broad internally (i.e. 32–54 square metres of floor space). Each house had a rubble or cobble stand at the north end, but no open drain or sump. This suggests the stabling of horses, rather than cattle, an interpretation supported by the discovery of horseshoes and nails and decorative brasses. Two fourteenth-century buildings had stone-lined and capped drains designed to aid the run-off of groundwater, necessary because the houses

Chest key.
A copper alloy chest key of the thirteenth century found during excavations at Springwood Park, Kelso. Increased security is typified on rural and urban sites by the use of padlocks on doors and shuttered windows and chest keys such as this one for personal belongings of value.
P.J. DIXON

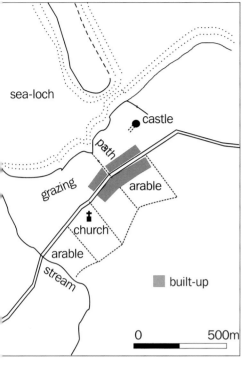

Rattray village.

Plan of the medieval village of Rattray, Aberdeenshire, showing the street layout of the thirteenth to fifteenth century.

(right)

Annular brooch.

This brooch is a functional object with little decoration. Annular brooches were a common method of pinning clothing in place, and they were often decorated. It might hold a cloak or plaid in place.

P.J.DIXON

were terraced into the ground. Only one hearth was encountered in this phase of occupation, therefore it is presumed that a brazier was used for cooking and heating, and that the hot ashes were swept out afterwards. Yet stone hearths appear to have been used in the thirteenth-century buildings – one building contained a complete example of a circular stone hearth. At least one house had a timber partition dividing the interior into two. A foundation trench for a timber partition was encountered in a thirteenth-century house. The sides were lined with small stones set on edge. These were intended to secure a timber into which the uprights of a partition could be set.

At Rattray the village tenements were spread out along a street about 500 metres long between the castle and the church. The only trace of the walls of the fourteenth–fifteenth-century peasant houses was a spread of clay more than 1 metre thick and up to 0.3 metres high. Grass impressions in the burnt area of one of the buildings suggests that the clay was mixed with grass, or possibly the presence of a turf wall. The scatters of stone at one end suggested a clay and stone gable to the excavators, but perhaps it was clay-boule, as at Springwood. The best of the Rattray buildings, the plan of which is an ill-defined rectangle, had entrances opposite each other in the middle of the long sides, which echoes at least one of the Springwood houses, and measured 3–4.5 metres broad by up to 18 metres long. Each entrance was about 1.5 metres wide and was flanked by a post-pit for a door jamb. A fire (fortuitous for the archaeologists, no doubt, but disastrous for the occupants) had preserved the charred remains of two collapsed roof timbers made of oak, 20–30 centimetres thick, possibly cruck-timbers, to one side of the entrance. On the other side of the entrance was a setting of small stones forming a box, which may mark the base for a timber partition.

The transition from post-set timber buildings to cruck-framed buildings

At Springwood prior to the thirteenth century and at Rattray prior to the fourteenth century the houses were based on earthfast timbers with no stone footing, but were probably clad with walls of turf. At Rattray a linear stain on a decayed timber sill-beam indicates that the walls of that building were built on timber beams laid on the ground. This form of architecture gave way to cruck-framing in the thirteenth century at Springwood and in the fourteenth century at Rattray, and although the number of excavated examples is small, it may be a general trend. There is no obvious explanation for the change, but a cruck-house (its walls primarily of stone or clay) required less timber which may indicate that there was less timber readily available, making suitable materials to build wattles for the walls more difficult to obtain. Such a shortage might follow the clearance of coppiced woodland – the main source of the long, thin poles needed.

An upland farmstead

Stone walls were also used at the upland farmstead of Dowglen in Eskdale, but we do not know what the walls were made of; they could have been of turf, and no cruck-settings were recognised. The farmstead comprised three platform-buildings on a steep slope above the improved fields that were formerly ridged. The buildings were 8–9 metres long, and up to 4.5 metres broad. The only internal features were a stone-capped drain along one side of one building, not unlike those at Springwood, and a possible rock-cut hearth. The lack of features makes it difficult to comment on the purpose of the buildings or the status of the inhabitants. The absence of artefacts also makes it difficult to date, although the complete absence of any post-medieval artefacts, such as clay pipes or bottle glass, suggests that the site was abandoned by the mid-1600s at the latest.

Excavations at Dowglen.
Platformed buildings under excavation at Dowglen in Eskdale, Dumfriesshire.
P.J. DIXON

Medieval Land Use: Farmland, Forest, Pasture and Woodland

'He lousit his pleuch at the landis en',
And draif his oxen hame at even;
When he come in he lookit ben,
And he saw the wife baith dry and clean,
And sittand at ane fire beikand bauld,
With ane fat soup as I heard say:
The man being very weet and cauld,
Between thae twa it was na play.'

The Wife of Auchtermuchty, Anon, 1568

Farmland and Cultivation

Medieval farming was a mixed enterprise in which the cultivation of land and the keeping of animals were equally important to success, though the balance varied from region to region. Cultivation provided those staple products of the Scottish peasant farmer, oats and barley. Domestic animals, sheep and cattle, provided milk, cheese and manure for the fields. The eastern seaboard from the Merse of Berwickshire to Moray was dry and warm enough to produce winter wheat as a cash crop, as well as the spring barley and oats, and for pasture to be relatively less important. The uplands of southern Scotland and the Highland fringe were more limited in potential for cultivation and had greater access to pasture. It was in these areas that the landlords of some lowland touns acquired upland grazings in order to provide the summer grazing they lacked. Lowland townships in the Merse used grazings on the Lammermuirs and in Aberdeenshire those in the Howe of Cromar had shielings in the glens of Strathdon on the edge of the Cairngorms.

Too often in the past, historians and archaeologists have viewed medieval agriculture as providing mere subsistence; however, the evidence from documents and by excavation suggests the development of a money economy. Peasants sold their surplus farm produce at the new burgh markets, and rents began to be paid more often in cash. By the late thirteenth century, the pre-feudal produce payments of *cain* and *conveth* were replaced by money, and labour services on the Kelso Abbey and Coldingham Priory estates were paid for in cash. Silver coins of different

Silver coins.
Silver coins from Springwood Park, Kelso. A range of silver coins, including cut-halfpennies and farthings, was recovered from this site and from Rattray in Aberdeenshire. This photo shows a silver penny and farthing of Edward I. English coins flooded into Scotland at this time.
P.J. DIXON

0   1 cm

omnis terra

Cantate domino ⁊ benedicite no
mini eius : annunciate de die in di

Fourteenth-century clod breaking.

The process of ploughing with a mould-board plough often left lumps of earth that needed to be broken up to provide a seed-bed. Clod braking with large mallets was a common rural practice in heavy soils prior to harrowing in Scotland as in England. BRITISH LIBRARY

denominations, pennies, cut-halfpennies and even a farthing were recovered from the village excavations at Springwood Park and Rattray. The concomitant need for security is indicated by a thirteenth-century copper-alloy chest key, a barrel padlock and key from Springwood Park, and by similar items from Rattray.

The changing face of agriculture as strip cultivation was spread northwards is shown by the way in which arable land is described in twelfth- and thirteenth-century charters. South of the Forth they include references to *oxgangs* (13 acres) and *carucates* (8 oxgangs). Carucates were divided into acres, and occasionally rigs (*reia*), and scattered in a variety of locations within the fields of a township (*villa*). These field-systems appear to be early examples of subdivided fields, later referred to as runrig (see Rig below). North of the Forth, and especially north of the Mounth, where the Grampians come down to the sea near Stonehaven, arable land was described in units called *davochs* or parts thereof. Each unit was individually named, suggesting that the davoch was a single holding, not subdivided into strips or rig. However, in the province between the Forth and the Mounth twelfth- and thirteenth-century records indicate that some arable lands were referred to as carucates as opposed to davochs. This may indicate the spread of rig northwards as new land was exploited, in which case the introduction of strip fields to Aberdeenshire may have occurred even later. Significantly, even if strip cultivation came relatively late to the north-east, rigs and butts (short rigs) are documented there by the post-medieval period, and are widely distributed on the ground.

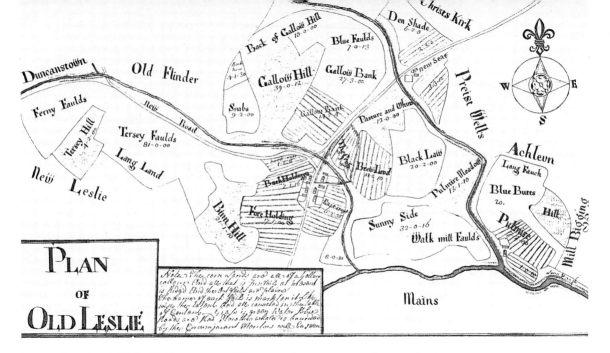

Eighteenth-century infield/outfield.

An estate map with field-names indicating
faulds or temporary outfield enclosures at
Old Leslie, Aberdeenshire, 1758. Note the
two-row village plan.

NATIONAL ARCHIVES OF SCOTLAND

There are, however, no references in the contemporary
documentation to land lying fallow, because this was not part of
agricultural practice. Examination of the lands sown on the home farm
(*demesne*) at Coldingham Priory in the fourteenth century shows a
fluctuation in the acreage sown from less than 100 acres to more than
300 acres. The fluctuations are partly related to disasters like the Black
Death and the devastation of Edward III's 1356 campaign. Yet *c.* 1298
the Priory had about 1000 acres of arable land in the demesne, which
suggests that the rest had either been let to tenants, or turned to
pasture; there is no mention of a fallow break.

The post-medieval infield-outfield system of agriculture is not
directly referred to in the documentation until the late fifteenth
century, although there are slightly earlier references to *outsets*, which
may be the same thing. The management of infield-outfield depended
on the occasional cultivation of areas of pasture in order to
supplement the produce of the infield. Medieval practice may have
allowed the temporary cultivation of the common pastures, in effect
outfield, without any necessity to document it, since it was temporary.
Its appearance in the documentation is a facet of the late and
post-medieval expansion in settlement that began in the later fifteenth
century. This brought pressure to make outfield permanent as new
settlements were established.

Rig

The creation of ridges for the purposes of cultivation prior to the
medieval period is now well-known. Prehistoric ridges appear to have
been raised with a combination of sod-busting plough and spade, and
were about 1–1.5 metres wide. Dating of the growth of peat over
some abandoned ridges of this kind indicates that they went out of use

in the course of the first thousand years AD, if not later. This dating also suggests that the notion of ridging was by no means foreign to medieval cultivators.

A ridge may be built by ploughing a strip of arable land spiral fashion with a mould-board plough from the centre outwards, turning the sod continually inwards, which, in time, builds up a ridge. Ridging is not a necessity in strip cultivation, but it may be a practical solution since otherwise each strip would require marking, a practice not unheard of in medieval records, which occasionally refer to marker stones (e.g. of Southrig in the *tenement* of South Hailes in East Lothian). Ridging with a mould-board plough created in time a visible unit that could be identified by its position in a furlong or block of rig. In subdivided fields this provided a practical solution to identifying a particular holding. One such holding is described in a charter of about 1200 for the township of *Balbotlia* (possibly Babbet) in Fife concerning the sale of a holding which comprised every fifth rig in the fields, suggesting that a system of juxtaposed rigs or strips was in operation. The Scots name for the distribution of rigs or strips in this way, where adjacent rigs might be held by different proprietors or tenants, is *runrig*, but it is not documented by this name until the fifteenth century.

At some point – we do not know exactly when – broad ridges became the standard method of cultivation over southern and eastern Scotland, from Roxburghshire to Sutherland in the far north. The documentary evidence above, and the use of Scandinavian field names, suggests that it may have been present in the south-eastern counties from the twelfth century, if not before, and was introduced into the counties between the Forth and the Mounth during the twelfth and thirteenth centuries, as new land was taken into cultivation.

We cannot prove that the broad ridges we can see surviving on the ground are the documented rig. However, there is no doubt that broad ridges, usually measuring in excess of 5 metres, and up to as much as about 15 or 20 metres wide, are to be found from Roxburghshire to Sutherland. The ridges are clearly distinguishable from the very narrow and much slighter prehistoric ridging described above, and from the low straight narrow Improvement Period ridges, generally 3–5 metres wide. Some ridges are grouped into blocks known as *butts* or *furlongs*, and can vary from 100 metres to more than 200 metres long according to the terrain; they are characterised by their high backs and curvilinear form, creating a reverse-S shape. The high back is presumably the result of longevity, as is the reverse-S shape. The high back is built up by the action of continually turning the sod in towards the centre of the ridge over a long period. The reverse-S shape is thought to be due to the use of a large oxen plough-team, which was pulled to the left at the end of the ridge in

Reverse-S rig.
This furlong of rig at Sheriffmuir in Perthshire has the typical, reverse-S shape of developed broad rig.
CROWN COPYRIGHT RCAHMS

Broad rig and terracing.
High-backed reverse-S rig at Braemoor
Knowe, Roxburghshire. The reverse-S
shape of broad rig is thought to be the
result of ploughing with a fixed heavy
mould-board plough. The sod is turned in
towards the centre of the strip, forming in
time a ridge, which is bent to the left at its
ends by the need to keep the plough biting
the soil as the plough team is turned. The
terraces are due to ploughing diagonally to
the slope, leading to soil slip.
CROWN COPYRIGHT RCAHMS

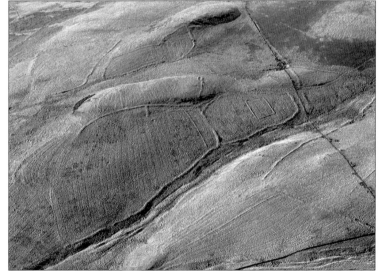

Undeveloped low rig.
An area of undeveloped rig at Menstrie
Glen, Stirlingshire. The earthen field-banks
are the remains of temporary faulds, and the
low rig is thought to be an area of outfield
cultivation.
CROWN COPYRIGHT RCAHMS

Spaded rig.
An area of narrow ridging at Auchensoul,
southern Ayrshire, with sharp profiled rigs
and discontinuities, indicating spade-
finished rig. Such rig is more common in
the South-west.
CROWN COPYRIGHT RCAHMS

order to keep the mould-board plough biting the sod as the team
began to turn.

There is a growing body of evidence from field survey for outfield
cultivation. Not all broad rig is high-backed and some, indeed, is
undeveloped, defined mainly by the groove of the furrow rather than
the ridge, suggesting that it reflects a short period of use. Since this
type of cultivation is particularly common on the fringes of cultivation
in south-east Scotland, and often shows signs of more than one
alignment of the furrows, it can be explained as outfield cultivation.
Another facet of outfield is the temporary enclosure or *fauld*, which is
documented from the sixteenth century. Indeed, earthen-banked
enclosures associated with undeveloped rig have been recognised on
the ground in recent years.

Archaeological excavation in the Lunan Valley, Angus, showed that

Curving narrow rig.
Curvilinear rig at Quarterside of Lipney,
Menstrie Glen, displaying an onion-peel
plan with the ridges narrowing at the ends.
This type of rig is from the Improvement
period when broad rigs were no longer
required, runrig having been abandoned.
CROWN COPYRIGHT RCAHMS

Danish ploughing experiment.
Attempts to understand the process of ridge ploughing with a heavy mould board plough were tried by Dr Grith Lerche in Denmark, using a wheel version not known to have been used in Scotland where the swing plough was common. Ridges showed little sign of formation in a single episode of ploughing.
G. LERCHE

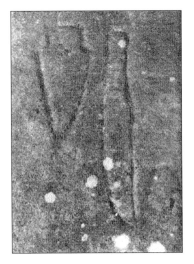

Plough irons.
A fourteenth-century grave-slab from Pennersaughs, Dumfriesshire, showing a pair of plough-irons, a coulter and a share or sock. Plough-irons, such as these, are referred to in the fourteenth-century inventory of Coldingham Priory.
CROWN COPYRIGHT RCAHMS

Old Scotch plough.
An surviving example of an Old Scotch plough from Aberdeenshire. The share and coulter are missing, but the brace for the coulter is visible on the stilt.
FENTON

one furlong of rig was formed in the late medieval period, while another at North Straiton, Fife, replacing a system of ditched plots, was dated after the thirteenth century. The spread of rig to the north-eastern counties is likely to be of similar date. Broad rig may be found in many parts of Aberdeenshire from the seaboard to the hills of upper Strathdon, and has also been recognised in Highland fringe townships in Sutherland straths such as Kildonan, Strathnaver and Rogart. However, a recent study has shown that other forms of ridging are evident in south-west Scotland, including so-called *lazy-bed rigs*, mainly found in patches in Galloway and southern Ayrshire. These rigs are usually relatively irregular and steep-edged and probably spade-dug.

Ploughs and farming implements

To create the high-backed ridges that decorate lowland Scotland with corrugations, a heavy mould-board plough or swing plough, known in the late eighteenth century as the old Scotch plough, was used. This plough, which required a large plough-team to pull it, had a substantial mould-board that helped turn the sod towards the centre of the ridge. As it did not have a wheel to support the front of the beam, as was common in south-east England, it depended on the skill of the ploughman to steer it effectively. The surviving examples at Peterhead and Stranraer Museums are largely wooden with an iron share and coulter. Plough-irons are referred to in an Inventory of Coldingham Priory of 1374 (see page oo) and presumably comprise a share and coulter, as depicted on the roughly contemporary grave-slabs from Pennershaughs, and Cummertrees, in Dumfriesshire. There is a good

deal of documentary evidence for the use of oxen to provide traction, but draught horses (*affri*) are also known and are listed in the Coldingham Inventory. Both draught horses and oxen are mentioned in documented grazing entitlements (*soums*) at places such as Mow in the Cheviots or Garvock in the Mearns of Kincardineshire. No ploughs have been found on excavations, although the iron tip of a ploughshare was found at Rattray.

Another key tool of cultivation was the spade. Iron tips from the rectangular wooden blade of a spade were found at Eyemouth in Berwickshire and from a pointed wooden blade at Perth. The best assemblage of agricultural tools from archaeological excavation comes from the burgh of Perth, reminding us of the rural interests of many urban dwellers. They include, in addition to the spade tip, sheep-shears, a sickle blade, a scythe blade and a hoe. These contrast with the list of tools in the 1374 Inventory of Coldingham Priory (see page 00), which includes sleds, threshing flails, hay forks and rakes, weeding tongs, three carts (two of which were iron-shod), two ploughs, a pair of plough-irons (presumably a share and coulter), and six harrows: the typical toolkit of the large farming operation. The spade, however, is *par excellence* the tool of the smallholder or cottar, who could not afford the draught animals needed for the heavy mould-board plough, but could benefit from the improved productivity of the more labour-intensive spade.

Crops

When the promoters of agricultural improvement in the late 1700s tried to persuade others of the need to change, they exaggerated the shortcomings of traditional farming. It is therefore easy to underestimate the medieval farmer. A variety of crops were grown in the medieval period, including winter wheat. Charred seeds from stratified deposits from the excavations at Springwood Park, Kelso, confirm the presence of oats, rye, bread wheat and hulled barley. Charred grain from medieval corn-drying kilns ranging from the late eleventh to the seventeenth century in Perthshire, Kincardineshire and West Lothian included oats and barley. Wheat was found at Chapelton in Angus and barley and wheat were identified at Kelso. At Lhanbryde in Moray, a grain-drier produced a large quantity of charred hulled oats, with smaller amounts of hulled barley, bread wheat, and rye. No obvious cropping pattern can yet be discerned in this, except that barley is almost universal and was probably malted in the kiln preparatory to brewing. To date, only the carbonised seeds from the kiln at Abercairny display any clear evidence of the germination that must have occurred in order for malted barley to have been produced. Wheat is present in eastern locations from the Borders to Moray. The growing of winter wheat suggests that there

Tools of cultivation.
An assemblage of agricultural tools from Perth: an iron tip for a wooden spade, sheep-shears, a sickle head, a scythe blade and a hoe.
PERTH MUSEUM

Fourteenth-century weeding.
This scene shows the weeding of corn using a weeding hook and crooked stick. Weeding hooks are referred to in the fourteenth-century inventory of Coldingham Priory.
BRITISH LIBRARY

was some division of cropping units in the fields, since barley and oats are generally spring-sown. Whether this was organised by group of adjacent rigs or by individual rig is not known.

Documentary evidence for the crops grown in the medieval period compares well with the distribution of archaeological evidence. Oats and barley were more common north of the Forth, with wheat occasionally referred to, but wheat was more often grown south of the Forth, as well as oats or barley. Oats and barley were staples; barley was used primarily for malt, and oats as the basis of oatmeal or for making bannocks, and also as fodder for horses. Wheat was used to make white bread, a desirable commodity in a monastery like Coldingham Priory.

In Coldinghamshire in the fourteenth century peas and beans were also regularly cultivated, usually in small quantities of a few acres, but occasionally much larger areas were sown which suggests they were

Fourteenth-century threshing.
The threshing of corn was carried out with a flail as shown here.
BRITISH LIBRARY

grown as a cash crop. At this period up to 80 acres of the Coldingham Priory demesnes were regularly sown with winter wheat, while between 100 and 200 acres were sown with barley and oats (generally with about four times as much oats as barley). The grand total of about 300 sown acres appears to be a very low figure, since there were 10 carucates, or in excess of 1000 acres of demesne arable at Coldingham in *c*.1300. This indicates either that the demesne was leased to tenants from the early fourteenth century, or that it was turned to pasture.

In addition to these cereals other crops were grown that were important to the economy. Teinds of hemp which could be used in the production of sacks, rope, canvas or nets were paid from most of the townships of Coldinghamshire in the fourteenth century, while pollen from the sediments in Yetholm Loch in the Cheviots and from Black Loch, near Lindores Abbey, Fife, also suggests that the growth of hemp was widespread in lowland Scotland. We also know from the sacristan's records that flax was grown and tithed on the Coldingham Priory estate. It was used as the raw material for linen shrouds, altar cloths, and priests' robes.

Pollen of alfalfa (lucerne), believed to date from the twelfth century, has been found in the infill of a ditch at Over Rig near Eskdalemuir in southern Scotland. Lucerne is generally thought to be a post-medieval innovation, therefore its recovery in such a context requires explanation. It could be that the Cistercians introduced it, as sometime between 1165 and 1169 they obtained part of Eskdale from Robert Avenel, a young man of Norman extraction who was granted Eskdale by David I in 1141. However, both the Cistercians and

Fourteenth-century sheep bucht.
A temporary pen constructed of wattles and fixed by loops of rope at the corners is being use to contain milk sheep in this fourteenth-century image of a sheep-bucht. The milking of sheep was common until the eighteenth century in Scotland and the turf-built pens that were used for this purpose are still littered across the hills of lowland Scotland.
BRITISH LIBRARY

Avenel would have had connections with continental European practice and may have known of lucerne's properties as a fodder crop and soil improver. A reference to lucerne in the Coldingham Inventory, records that a few acres were sown in conjunction with wheat; this does not suggest use of lucerne as a fallow crop, but rather that it was undersown with wheat to improve the yield.

Farm animals

At present there is little evidence for domestic animals from rural settlement sites. The acid soils of Scotland do not preserve bone well, although sites of manorial status have produced assemblages. The survival of bone at Springwood Park village, for example, was poor – it was mainly the larger bones and teeth that survived. This may bias the sample to the more robust cattle bone at the expense of sheep. Indeed, cattle bone was more common than sheep, and there were indications that pigs were also kept in small numbers. In contrast, sheep bones predominate at castle sites such as Edinburgh Castle, urban sites of the south-east, and at Eyemouth village in Berwickshire. This supports the documentary evidence that in terms of numbers sheep were the most important farm animal on the monastic estates of Kelso, Melrose and Coldingham. In contrast, the excavation of urban sites further north such as Aberdeen and Perth have produced a much greater representation of cattle bone.

The importance of wool in animal husbandry is to be found in the bone assemblages from Rattray and Eyemouth. At both sites few sheep were under two years old at death, and most were kept to a mature age; this indicates that sheep were kept for wool production rather than meat and also perhaps for milk.

Despite their numbers at these sites, the larger carcass size of cattle ensured that beef was a much more substantial source of meat. Cattle at Eyemouth and Rattray were also kept to maturity, although the implications of this is a matter of dispute. At Eyemouth it was suggested that the herds were kept for dairying and traction, whereas at Rattray this was considered unlikely because of the low numbers of slaughtered young, which would have been needed for milk production. However, this absence may also be explained by the export of stirks to the markets of Aberdeen down the coast. Pigs formed a small but regular part of the domestic herd. At Eyemouth and Rattray this was less than one-tenth of the bones, similar to urban sites. Unlike sheep and cattle, the entire value of pigs was in their meat and the few that were kept beyond their second year were presumably breeding stock. Small quantities of horse bones from what appear to have been small draught ponies, 12–14 hands high, are represented at Eyemouth, Rattray and Springwood Park.

By comparison, the Coldingham Priory records of the fourteenth and early fifteenth centuries are a particularly useful source of information on animal husbandry and indicate that the Priory kept a flock that, at its maximum, exceeded 2000 sheep. It has been calculated that Melrose Abbey had in excess of 12,000 sheep in its flocks. Coldingham also maintained a cattle herd of up to 180 in a good year so that ratios of sheep to cattle on this estate were often greater than 10:1. The 1374 Inventory records that stirks were kept to three years of age, and that there were 42 cows, 34 draught oxen and three draught horses. It is not clear, however, if the draught horses were for pulling sleds, wagons or ploughs, all of which are listed in the same Inventory. Pigs were a small but regular element in the herd, at between 30 and 60 animals, and, as was found at the excavated sites, were mostly young rather than mature animals.

Pasture

Evidence for pasture is hard to pin down archaeologically, except from the presence of structures related to animal management. As well as shielings, medieval records occasionally mention sheep houses, and byre houses such as those built by Melrose Abbey between the Gala and Leader waters, or folds for sheep management as recorded by Kelso Abbey at Stapelaw in Mow in the Cheviots. The documents contain many references to the granting of grazing rights, many of which were designed to provide pasture for draught animals, as well as herds of sheep and cattle. Pasture for pigs in wooded areas called pannage is also documented.

The right to build a shieling – shelter at a summer grazing – did not automatically go with grazing, since such constructions might be used to establish a permanent settlement, which might be against the interest of the landlord. The shieling might include a domestic shelter and other structures such as a dairy or milking shed. These temporary huts are the most readily recognisable feature of the landscape. Many examples of shieling huts have been recorded in the upland fringes of the lowlands from the Cheviots northwards. Most are to be found alongside a burn near a regular source of water and the best grazing. Walled with turf or stone or a combination of the two, they are generally shorter and narrower than the houses on permanent sites, and unlike them often have a midden heap outside the entrance. Lowland examples have been excavated at Muirkirk in Ayrshire, which produced medieval pottery.

Hunting Forest

Traditionally in Scotland anyone could hunt an animal if it was on their land: the medieval hunting forest was a new departure in Scotland that ran counter to this. By introducing the hunting forest,

Sixteenth-century huntsman.

An image from a sixteenth-century book of Robin Hood. This gives a good impression of a medieval huntsman on his horse, a strong, short and sturdy beast, well-equipped for the rugged terrain or draught work that probably typifies the medieval style of horse in Scotland.

NATIONAL LIBRARY OF SCOTLAND

Assart enclosure.

This assart at Martinlee Sike, Southdean, in the forest of Jedburgh, comprises about 7 hectares in area within a curvilinear dyke on the Carter Burn. Ridge and furrow and two farmsteads, probably of different periods, are visible within it.

J. DENT

the king was reserving the deer in particular to himself in a royal forest. On baronial estates such as Annandale or Liddesdale the grant of free forest gave the baron the right to hunt deer on behalf of the king. This was a clever move that appears to have largely avoided the kind of clashes that emerged in England, where the king set up hunting forests over whole counties and tried to maintain his rights to the exclusion of all others. Even so, it was a new system of management that laid down penalties for poaching deer, and for any activities liable to adversely affect the habitat of the deer, known as the *vert*, a suitable mixture of woodland and open grazing. Agriculture and the grazing of domestic animals in a forest required a licence, as did any other kind of economic exploitation of the land of the forest. Whilst the prime motive was to secure royal hunting rights, in practice it did not prevent the expansion of settlement and agriculture, or the exploitation of pasture and woodland, but gave the king or baron control over the process.

In the twelfth, thirteenth and early fourteenth centuries in Annandale, Renfrewshire, Roxburghshire, and elsewhere, intakes of arable in the forest, known as *assarts* from the French 'to grub up trees', were licensed. This effectively deforested land from the hunting reserve. Indeed, the grant of assart usually specified the right to enclose and hedge as well cultivate the assart. Since the grants of assart were for pieces of land that now lie in modern farmland, the physical remains of this process are hard to find. Where the pressures to settle

and farm land were sufficiently strong, forest law appears to have presented little practical limitation to improvement.

In Liddesdale, right on the English border, a rental of 1376 lists the farms in the four quarters of the dale and a fifth area called the forest. Clearly the actual forest by this time covered a much reduced area from the whole lordship to which the free forest extended. Examination of the place names of land being rented in the forest at this time, presumably for grazing, finds the greater part lay in the hill country on the north and west of the dale. The rest of the dale was occupied mainly by forest farms, called *steads*, and a few places, which by their names suggest a toun or larger settlement. There are no documented assarts in Liddesdale, although there were some in the hunting forest that lay on the English side of the border. However, field survey has revealed extensive enclosures defined by a dyke comprising a bank and external ditch. Individual intakes of land from the forest could take in several hundred hectares as on Kirkhill to the

Deer-Trap

Artificial deer-traps, comprising, in this case, palisaded dykes, provided a killing ground for a deer hunt in a royal or baronial hunting forest in the twelfth and thirteenth centuries.
DAVID SIMON

Deer trap.
An aerial photograph of the narrow end of a V-shaped deer-trap beside Hermitage Castle, Roxburghshire. The arms of the trap come together at right angles to one another just outside the modern stone dyke surrounding the castle.
CROWN COPYRIGHT RCAHMS

Assart dyke.
An example of an assart dyke at Martinlee Sike, Southdean, in the forest of Jedburgh in Roxburghshire. Note the external ditch highlighted by the stone dyke that rides down into it.
CROWN COPYRIGHT RCAHMS

south of Newcastleton, or just a few acres as at Greenshiels to the north. The intakes included both arable land and pasture. Since the Liddesdale intakes are not documented, they were probably carried out by unfree tenants of the estate, whose licences to assart may have been entered in manorial records, none of which survive.

Surviving grants of assart gave the right to cultivate and build a farm within the assart, but did not necessarily provide any rights to graze or cut peat on the common land. Paisley Abbey, for example, was granted an assart by Walter the Steward in his forest of Renfrew in which they could 'plough and build, make hedges and enclosures saving my wildfowl and beasts', but they were to be fined if they allowed their animals into the forest, especially in the close season. However, they were allowed to get timber for building and fuel, and pannage for 100 pigs in the autumn when the oak mast fell.

What is known of the methods used by the Scots nobility to hunt deer? The use of hounds in the chase dates back to Pictish times. The hounds were specially trained and controlled by means of a swivel lead, which allowed several dogs to be tethered to one huntsman. An example of such a lead was found at Rattray. The deer were driven by a large team of huntsmen and their dogs into an *elrig* or natural trap from which escape was difficult. The trapped animals were then shot with bows and arrows. The deer could have been red, roe or fallow, all of which have been recovered from the excavations at Rattray.

Recent survey has revealed a man-made type of deer-trap, not strictly a park in the sense of a complete enclosure. This type of trap is essentially an *elrig* enhanced by the construction of a deer-dyke. The common characteristic of these deer-traps is the way in which they use the lie of the land: a natural gully or declivity is enclosed on three sides, leaving the easy approach to the gully open. Two new traps have been located in the Scottish borders, at Hermitage Castle in

Liddesdale and in Hownam parish in the heart of the Cheviots. At Hermitage the deer-dyke comprises a funnel-shaped arrangement of dykes on either side of a stream gully to the north-west of the castle. Hownam, which was also the subject of the grant of a hunting forest, is remarkable for having a deer-dyke that is in part built as a stone revetment that still stands to about 1 metre high. Both are open on one side. This also appears to be the case with the northern extension at Kincardine Park, which lay near the site of the royal castle of Kincardine. The construction of the park is documented from 1264 to 1266, although it may have earlier origins. The park comprised two parts: the southern part appears to have been an enclosed area straddling the Garrol Burn some 2 miles across, although the south side no longer survives in the modern farmland; the northern extension was a trap that enclosed the gully of the Arnbarrow Burn on three sides, but was open to the east. The northern extension is accessible from the main park enclosure via a narrow gap, which appears to match the narrow gap in the trap at Hermitage Castle.

An improvement on the hunting forest was the hunting park, another Anglo-Norman innovation. The park was a large enclosure built to keep deer in a reserve for hunting. The enclosure, which was designed to facilitate the entry of deer but prevent their escape, comprised a palisaded bank and an internal ditch, although no

Park pale.
A medieval park pale at Buzzart Dikes, Perthshire is visible riding over the ridge in the foreground. The ditch in an enclosed deer park was on the inside of the dyke which was surmounted by a fence or paling.

The Inventory of the Priory of Coldingham, 1374

The following is extracted and translated from the inventory of Coldingham Priory in 1374, as transcribed by Reverend James Raine and published by the Surtees Society in 1841. The chapel, chamber, hall, accounting house, cloth store, wine cellar, brewery, and kitchen are not itemised here as they related mainly to the conventual life rather than the home farm and rural life. The items here should be viewed as typifying the home farm of monastic estates and so is better equipped than peasant farms, but it does show the range of equipment and produce that could be found in lowland Scotland at this period.

In the Larder

25 salted beef and 8 salted cow carcasses.
24 salted salmon.
2 boxes of white herring (dried?).
16 vats of soused herring (doukdrawis).
42 stockfish, or dried cod/ling.
13 measures of red herring (smoked?).

In the Granary

4 quarters of wheat from our field.
Item 2 chalders and 1 boll of barley.
Item 10 chalders of oats, apart from sheaves of fodder for the prior's horses and plough-oxen, and for two beef cattle fattened for the kitchen.
Item 4 chalders and 2 bushels of malted barley,
2 boxes of wheat-flour.
Item containers sufficient for the granary.

On the Farm

3 draught horses.
1 heifer.
34 oxen for ploughs and wagons.
3 wagons provided with all necessary equipment of which 2 are shod with iron.
Item 52 acres of alfalfa sown with wheat,
2 cupboards.
Item 1 pair of new wheels for the wagons.
Item 2 ploughs with equipment,
1 pair of plough-irons,
6 harrows,
2 sledges, flails, forks, hay-rakes,
1 pair of weeding tongs, and other tools necessary for husbandry.
Item 6.5 iron bars of unworked iron.
Item 5 sows and 1 boar.
Item 7 boxes of tar for sheep.

In the Stable

1 riding horse and 1 pack-horse.

In the Smithy

1 pair of bellows, 1 great anvil (stotsteyt), 1 small anvil, 2 forehammers, 2 hand-hammers, 1 nail-making tool, 1 pair of tongs.
In the Timber Store
58 wooden boards cut for roof tiles.
Item at Coldingham 64 uncut boards.
Item 95 oak spars.
Item 11 pine spars.
Item 6300 double nails.
Item 2000 single nails, 50,000 brods, 200 spikes, 500 clench-bolts.
Item 8 chalders of lime for repairing houses.
Item two 24 foot rolls of lead.
[boats and stores at Berwick, Eyemouth and the port of Coldingham are excluded here]

In the Byre

7 bulls.
Item 42 cows.
Item 17 three-year old bullocks.
Item 9 two-year old bullocks.
Item 13 calves.

Sheep

2214 sheep.
Rent of farms [erased].
Item mills [erased].
Item teinds [erased]

Collection of Tithes.
Tithes being collected in the Outer Court
pof the monastery at Coldingham Priory.
Sheaves are being taken into the granary on
the left of the picture.
DAVID SIMON

excavation has taken place to confirm this. A few parks are documented in the twelfth and thirteenth centuries, mainly royal parks such as those at Stirling, Jedburgh, or Kincardine. Neither of the first two has been located on the ground, but the Kincardine park is very clearly defined. In the fourteenth and fifteenth centuries parks became more common as the pressure on land in the hunting forests for agricultural use competed with the demands of the chase.

Scottish medieval parks have received little attention from archaeologists. Most lie in areas of modern farmland and, apart from the farm names, have left little trace on the landscape. An undocumented park was recorded within the forest of Clunie at Buzzart Dyles in Perthshire. It comprised a roughly rectangular area enclosed by an earthen bank and internal ditch on three sides and a short length of the return of each side at the other end. Significantly, the enclosure cuts across two natural gullies, so that there were suitable locations for trapping deer within the park.

Woodland Exploitation and Woodland Management

By the medieval period, the countryside of lowland Scotland was already an open farmed landscape. Woodland was localised and probably managed, although coppicing and pollarding are not explicitly described in the documentary sources. Coppicing involves the cutting of poles from a tree stool at just above ground level, while pollarding cuts the poles from higher up, well above the reach of grazing animals, which produces thin poles that are used in the construction of wattles or hurdles for fencing or buildings. Most of the records are about the exploitation of woods and only occasionally about its conservation. Equally, wattles recovered from archaeological sites have yet to produce convincing evidence for management, as opposed to opportunistic exploitation.

Documented woodland is usually recorded from the point of view of its exploitation. Lindores Abbey took dead wood for fires and 200 loads of hazel rods from the wood of Tulyhen for making sleds and hoops, the Bishop of Glasgow obtained oak for building the cathedral from the oak woodland at Luss, the tenants of Cupar Angus Abbey in Atholl took wood for the repair of ploughs, carts, harrows and fencing, and similar rights were given to Kelso Abbey in the wood called the Scrogges in the Bowmont Valley of the Cheviots.

Charcoal-burning.
A coppiced oak wood at Loch Awe, Argyllshire, containing a level circular platform for making charcoal. The stump is cut close to the ground and the shoots allowed to grow to suitable size for harvesting.
P.J. DIXON

However, recent documentary research has started to reveal the extent of post-medieval management of woodland, including coppicing and the enclosure of woodland to exclude unwanted animals. The Norse terminology used for many of its activities suggests that an old tradition of woodland management was already well established by the seventeenth century and has early medieval origins.

A well-documented use for woodland is for pannage or grazing for pigs in autumn. Pannage suggests that a form of wood pasture was operating. Although the deposition of acorns or beech nuts (and beech is not a common tree in medieval Scotland) is an irregular business in Scotland, because of the climate, pannage is nonetheless a documented activity in the twelfth century.

Ancient examples of coppiced oak stools survive in Methven Wood, Perthshire, and Mugdock Wood near Glasgow, and there are multiple-trunked oaks of considerable antiquity in Dalkeith Park near Edinburgh which are difficult to date precisely. The size of the coppice poles can be used to estimate the time since the last coppice event, but dating the stump is less easy.

Ancient pollarded trees, with their characteristic candelabra shape, are more rewarding as evidence of the management of old woodland. Some of the gnarled oaks of Cadzow Oaks, Hamilton, some of which lie in Châtelherault Park, and those at Dalkeith Park appear to have pollard features. However, examination of the Cadzow oaks only found a handful with convincing evidence for the reduced growth in the tree rings that may be expected to follow a pollarding. Some idea of the antiquity of these trees is given by the dating of a Cadzow oak stump by dendrochronology to AD 1444, and it has been suggested that the girth of some of the trees indicates that they could be even older. Their survival has been helped by their location in an ornamental park. Ancient oaks in parkland will have been selectively maintained since medieval times as much for their appearance as for their use as a source of wood. Unlike coppiced trees, access to which

Pigs and pannage.
Modern pigs grazing in woodland. Pannage
was the grazing of managed oak woodland
by pigs for its acorn harvest. It is most
frequently documented in the twelfth and
thirteenth centuries in Scotland.
FORESTRY COMMISSION

needs to be limited until they are well-established, stock can continue
to be grazed in pollarded woods.

The use of woodland for charcoal manufacture is not well
documented until the post-medieval period, when it was associated
with iron smelting. Many other industrial processes such as salt
making, corn drying, pottery production, lead smelting, and bronze
casting benefit from the improved heat generated by charcoal, as
opposed to peat, or wood faggots. The woods of Callender near
Falkirk were used as a source of fuel to provide the heat for salt-pans,
but no mention is made of charcoal. It has yet to be demonstrated that
charcoal burning was a medieval industry in Scotland, and the use of
the word 'coal' for charcoal may be open to misinterpretation. Place
names such as Colstoun in East Lothian are perfectly explicable as
being derived from the outcropping of coal rather than from charcoal
burning, while the carriage of 'coal' from Berwick by tenants of Kelso
Abbey is also likely to be coal, as it outcrops just south of Berwick.

Peat-cutting

Peatbogs, a ubiquitous part of Scotland's countryside then as now,
were more extensive in the medieval period; former peatbogs such as
the Carse of Gowrie or the Carse of Stirling and the periphery of
Flanders Moss have been extensively drained and the peat cover
removed.

Peat was widely used as a fuel for domestic purposes. It may also
have been used for firing corn-drying kilns, and we have evidence
that it was used as fuel in the pottery kilns at Rattray. It was also a
cheap fuel to use in salt-pans. It is documented that a whole host of
monasteries, Jedburgh, Cambuskenneth, Holyrood, Dunfermline and
Newbattle gained access to peat on the Carse of Stirling to provide
fuel for their nearby salt-pans. These have yet to be located.

Rural Industry

'Than to the kirn that he did stoure,
And jumlit at it whill he swat,
When he had jumlit a full lang hour,
The sorrow crap of butter he gat.
Albeit na butter he could get,
Yit he was cummerit with the kirn,
And syne he let the milk owre het,
And sorrow spark of it wald yirn.'

The Wife of Auchtermuchty, Anon, 1568

Introduction

Many of the rural crafts and industries of the medieval countryside, including those domestic crafts based on animal products (such as wool) and on cereal products, were carried out by the cottars and labourers who lived and worked there. Specialised settlements for industrial workers have not been found. Fishermen also engaged in agriculture, potters located their potteries in the 'touns' and market 'touns', and were also likely to be agricultural tenants. Although some activities, such as the need to locate coal, silver, lead, iron or stone, drove prospectors into the rough pasture areas, there is little evidence that they set up permanent settlements to exploit them.

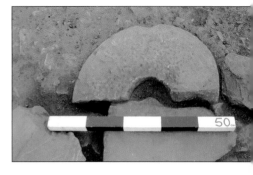

Millstone.
A broken millstone of thirteenth-century date from Springwood Park, Kelso, Roxburghshire.
P.J. DIXON

Corn-drying kiln.
An example of a medieval corn-drying or malting kiln from the excavations at Roxburgh Street, Kelso. This kiln was last used in the sixteenth century and had been used for both barley and wheat. As with most medieval grain-drying kilns, it was dug into the ground, making it easy to load the temporary floor at ground level. The grain was probably dried on the sheave, laid on an open floor of rafters, burnt examples of this process have been recovered in excavation.
P.J. DIXON

The Preparation of Cereal Products

Oats and barley provided meal and malt, the chief staples of the peasant. Both were controlled by the manor – grain had to be milled in the lord's mill, the lord keeping a proportion (*thirlage*), and ale brewed at the lord's brewery.

Grain milling

Oatmeal was one of the basic foodstuffs of the medieval period, but before it could be consumed it had to be dried and milled. Similarly, wheat was milled into flour which was used to make white bread for those lucky enough to be able to afford it. The feudal control of milling and the imposition of thirlage are well-documented elements of the medieval countryside, as is the taking of *multure*, a cut of the grain, by the miller as payment in kind for his services. Most estates possessed a mill to which the tenants were thirled, and there are frequent references to dams, lades, or stanks for the mills, being maintained by the tenants.

In the 1230s, Alan de Sinton wished to build a mill on the Esk near Edinburgh and had to promise that his mill would not impede the abbey of Dunfermline's mill by back-flood, which seems to imply the construction of a mill downstream on the same river; it also tells us that the abbey mill was undershot. Until the nineteenth century, mills were either undershot or breastshot, i.e. the water struck the wheel at the bottom or in the middle.

Not all mills were grain mills. From the 1200s, fulling or waulk mills, in which cloth was shrunk with fuller's earth, are documented. These mills also relied on water power. We do not know if water power was used in any other industrial process. Windmills are occasionally referred to in documents, as at Coldingham in 1305 – 'Wynmillraw' – but they were a new type of power source in England in the twelfth century, and presumably also in Scotland.

Despite frequent mention in documents, there is little

Water-mill
The vertically-driven mill, usually for grain, was a technological development of the medieval period in lowland Scotland. The mill was typically undershot as in this reconstruction.
DAVID SIMON

archaeological evidence of mills, probably because the river-banks
where the mills stood have eroded. To date, only one medieval mill,
in the burgh of Glasgow, has been excavated, which appears to have
been an undershot vertical mill. The mill was built entirely of
perishable materials on an earthfast timber frame with a porch on one
side. Whether this mill was typical cannot be known until more
examples come to light. Part of a mill-lade was excavated at
Lhanbryde in Moray, in which a corn-drying kiln was later
constructed (see below).

Millstones have been found on several medieval sites, often being
used as bases of furnace hearths as at Castlehill of Strachan in
Aberdeenshire. Several broken millstones were found at Springwood
Park, including one serving a similar function to that at Strachan. The
implication is that there was a mill nearby, as was recorded at Maxwell
near Kelso, Roxburghshire, in 1381–82. The getting of millstones was
a minor medieval industry. Throughout Scotland numerous coarse
sandstone outcrops were exploited. These are recognisable by the
rough-outs and millstone-shaped cuts in the rocky outcrops.

Corn-drying and malting

To make grain such as wheat and oats suitable for milling
it had to be dry enough to grind. Barley, which was
most frequently used in brewing, had to be
germinated and malted (i.e. the germinated
seed had to be scorched to prevent further
germination). Both processes needed a kiln.
In only one instance is there clear-cut
evidence for malting from the germinated
state of the barley. Although brewing is a
well-documented rural activity with
brewhouses figuring widely in medieval
rentals and charters, none have been
located archaeologically. Barley was also
perhaps used as the raw material for
whisky, but there is little medieval evidence
for stills.

Corn-drying
The drying of grain preparatory to milling
was an essential part of grain production in
Scotland. Most medieval kilns were set into
a terrace or pit in the ground, so that the
drying floor was at ground level, and the
superstructure was a thatched conical roof.
DAVID SIMON

Corn-drying kilns are one of the more frequent finds in rural
settlement. Documentary references to kilns, however, are rare.
Following harvest, the grain was gathered in sheaves. There is
documentation for teinds of grain being paid in this form at
Coldingham Priory in the fifteenth century. However, the corn
delivered to Roxburgh Castle by the tenants of Maxwell in 1266 had
to be thrashed and winnowed to be made ready for milling, which
suggests that it was stored on the sheaf.

A number of kilns have been excavated in both rural and urban

Glazed storage jar.
A large late twelfth- or early thirteenth-century jug with a hole drilled in its base. The base was set in the ground in a work area when broken, possibly to serve as a strainer for draining the whey from cheese.
P.J. DIXON

Loom weight and spindle whorls.
A loom weight for keeping the warp of a vertical loom taut found during excavations at Springwood Park, Kelso, Roxburghshire, and spindle whorls for spinning yarn.
P.J. DIXON

Leather shoes.
Leather shoes from the medieval midden in a lead mine at Sillar Holes, Peeblesshire. The midden excavated in a quarry pit at this site has rare examples of cloth and leather from a rural context.
TRUSTEES OF THE ROYAL MUSEUM OF SCOTLAND

(far right)
Woollen sleeve.
A sleeve from a woollen garment found in the medieval midden at Sillar Holes, Peeblesshire. The colours used in the cloth from this site were mainly drab browns.
TRUSTEES OF THE ROYAL MUSEUM OF SCOTLAND

contexts. They are lined with stone, turf or wattles. The kiln is either set into a steep slope or comprises a keyhole-shaped pit with steps down into it (e.g. Roxburgh Street, Kelso) and often take advantage of convenient man-made or natural mounds, for example, the counterscarp bank of Doune of Invernochty in Strathdon. The kiln-chamber is usually round with an opening or flue leading off from one side to the fire-chamber. Both kiln-chamber and flue are often lined in the same way, giving rise to the common keyhole shape. The kiln is typically about 1.5 metres deep and it is presumed that the chamber was floored at its top with timber beams, as suggested by the burnt timbers excavated at Capo, then covered with a permeable material such as wattles. Experiments with a grain-drying kiln at the Highland Folk Museum suggest that the sheaves can be laid directly on the beams without any covering, thus making it less likely that grains will be lost in the process, since there is no need to spread and rake loose grains. The burnt remains of undressed timbers found in the kiln at Capo suggest some form of roofing structure, which might have consisted of cruck-trusses, supporting rafters and a covering of thatch or heather.

The Processing of Animal Products

Not much of the carcass of sheep or cattle went to waste – wool, skin and bone were all usable in some way or other. The advantage of animals was that they were moveable wealth, which could be taken to market on the hoof. The major burghs were the centres for the buying, selling and processing of domestic animals and the manufacture of animal products such as leather. Unlike grain, which was essentially a staple product for the daily consumption of the peasantry, animals represented income, a source of labour and transport.

Spinning and weaving

One of the most common rural crafts was the preparation of yarn from sheep's wool or flax to make woollen or linen garments. Cloth, leather, rope and wood have been found amongst midden material, possibly of twelfth–fourteenth-century date, dumped in what may be a quarry hole for lead mining at Sillar Holes, Peeblesshire. The fragments of cloth include plain weave and twills comparable with those found in Aberdeen and Perth. Spindle whorls, heckle teeth and a loom weight were found at Springwood, indicating that more than one kind of cloth was produced there. Heckles were used to comb the wool prior to spinning when a worsted cloth was to be manufactured. The loom weight comes from a vertical loom. The dyes used on the cloth at Sillar Holes for mainly appear to be derived from woad and weld, dyer's rocket, both of which grow naturally in Scotland and release indigo and yellow respectively. Most of the colours used on the cloths, however, were variants on brown, although one sample used a red derived from cochineal, an imported insect-derived pigment.

Peasant house

Inside a peasant house, humans and animals lived cheek-by-jowl. The hearth was the focus, used both for heating and cooking, and spinning and weaving were common daily pursuits.
DAVID SIMON

Cheese-making

Cheese is often referred to in the documentation of peasant produce. It was used as tithe (*teind*) or as early medieval produce payments, such as *cain*, and even as rent at Monymusk Priory in Aberdeenshire. In the absence of cold storage, making cheese was the best way to preserve surplus milk from sheep and cattle. As cows and ewes would not have been in permanent lactation, the output of cheese was seasonal, often a product of the summer shieling. Archaeological evidence for cheese-making is not easy to come by. In the early-modern period, stone cheese presses were often found at farmsteads, but none have been recognised on the few medieval excavations to date.

The separation of curds and whey can be carried out in any vessel that allows the liquid to drain. If the cheese is to be kept, the curds must be pressed to remove the whey, producing a harder product that keeps longer. At Springwood the base of a broken jug which may have served as the base for a cheese press was set in the ground in

Yair

Tidal races were used to catch fish on many parts of the Scottish coast. The trap or yair comprised a permeable fence, which might be of wattles and stone, designed to trap fish in a pool.

DAVID SIMON

Fish-trap.

A fish-trap, comprising a wattled fence and dry-stone dyke, in the estuary of the Conon near Dingwall. The dry-stone dyke is often the only survival, but here the post-settings survived. This is one of many fish-traps that were built in the intertidal zone on the coast of Scotland in the medieval and post-periods. Others were built in rivers to catch fish that swim upstream to spawn.

CROWN COPYRIGHT HISTORIC SCOTLAND

what appears to be an outside work area. A small hole had been drilled through its wall near its base – the cheese would have been weighted with a flat stone and the surplus liquid would have drained through the hole.

Fishing

In Scotland there were few fish ponds for the breeding of freshwater fish, probably because of the proximity of the sea and the ease of access to sea fish such as salmon and sea-trout in the rivers. Fish, particularly salmon, was certainly part of the diet of monastic and lay tables with the Friday fast. However, other fish were preserved as stock-fish (dried cod or ling), or doukdrawis (possibly a type of soused fish). Herring were widely consumed, probably either dried or smoked, referred to as 'white' and 'red' herring respectively in the 1374 Coldingham Inventory.

Fish were caught in traps designed to take advantage of tidal firths and creeks, or by line and draw-net fishing at sea. Fish-hooks found in the medieval midden at Eyemouth are indicative of deep-sea line fishing for cod and ling, which were butchered for salting and drying. The lines were baited with sea molluscs such as limpets. However, herring, difficult to identify in archaeological sites because of the small bones, must have been caught using nets. Medieval boats are likely to have been open cobbles, perhaps with a single sail.

Fish traps, known as *yair* in Scots or *cruive* in Gaelic, were constructed of netting, or of wattle fences, or of stone with wattle retaining walls and have been found all around the coast of Scotland. They were designed to benefit from tidal races in estuaries trapping fish on the retreating tide. The trapped fish were then caught in nets or wickerwork creels set in a gap in the trap. The stone dyke is often the most readily visible in the intertidal zone, but recent surveys of the zone have begun to reveal examples of wattle fences, as in an example on the River Conon at Dingwall in Ross-shire.

Pottery Manufacture

The widespread use and occurrence of new types of pottery for household activities is one of the defining archaeological characteristics of the medieval period. From the twelfth century, ceramic vessels began to be widely used for cooking and for holding liquid. These new ceramics were made in the countryside, close to the clay source, and mainly for local use; they have been found on both lowland rural and urban sites and also in upland shielings, such as those near Muirkirk in Ayrshire. However, not all areas were within reach of a supply of clay pots. The settlement at Dowglen in Eskdale, for example, apparently had no ceramic vessels.

White Gritty Ware is found over much of eastern and southern Scotland, whereas to the north of Fife, pottery, known as Redwares on account of their colour, is most common. The Redwares of Perth were coated with a white slip to achieve a light-coloured finish similar to White Gritty Ware. This suggests a preference for the finish of the White Wares. Production sites for Redware have been found at Rattray, Aberdeenshire, and Stenhouse, Stirlingshire, but only one White Gritty Ware production site is yet known, at Colstoun, East Lothian.

Pottery production was one of the rural industries that appears to have been transformed in the twelfth century. This may be attributed to the influx of new technologies that followed in the wake of the reformed Benedictine orders such as the Cistercians. The pottery kilns at Rattray were located within a tenement in the village and date to the thirteenth and fourteenth centuries. The kilns were double-flued, comprising lined oval pits with flues opening opposite each other. At Colstoun the pottery is also at a rural site, probably within the context of a settlement, but a fourteenth-century kiln at Colstoun was a three-flued structure, indicating technological improvement.

Most of the Colstoun pottery was not intended as tableware. The pots were generally white-fired with occasional splashes of lead glaze giving a pale green finish to the shoulders of vessels such as jugs. Flat-bottomed vessels were rare and the pots had straight or curved sides. The vessels ranged from deep open bowls to pipkins, small pots

Pottery kiln
Pottery kilns being loaded and fired. The manufacture of everyday ceramic vessels was a rural industry, requiring clay for the vessels and kiln, and wood or peat for firing.
DAVID SIMON

Red Ware pottery kilns.
Successive pottery kilns at Rattray,
Aberdeenshire, producing Red Ware
pottery. Two of these are of two-flue
design, the openings of the flues lying at
opposite sides of the kiln. The kilns were
fired with peat.
CROWN COPYRIGHT HISTORIC SCOTLAND

Cooking pot.
A straight-sided twelfth-century cooking
pot from Kelso Abbey, Roxburghshire.
Globular forms of cooking pot were also
common.
TRUSTEES OF THE ROYAL MUSEUM OF
SCOTLAND

with short handles bent over at the end designed for pouring out
liquid. Large squat jugs were also common. Some were decorated
with face-masks, and most had strapped rather than cylindrical handles.

In the late fifteenth or early sixteenth century this changed.
Ceramic cooking vessels disappeared, suggesting that non-ceramic
materials such as metal were now being used. More tableware began
to be produced – jugs, bowls and dishes with flat-bottoms. These
usually had an all-over green glaze, and were generally fired in an
oxygen-free atmosphere which meant that the kiln had to be closed
efficiently during the final stage of firing. This is a different kiln
technology from that which produced the White and Red wares, and
is thought to indicate the onset of mass production. Stoneware
drinking vessels or frilly-based mugs, typically imported from the
Rhineland, also became common from around 1350. To date, the
only known sixteenth- and seventeenth-century pottery production
site is at Throsk in Stirlingshire.

Ironworking

The getting of iron was an important medieval industry and one which
was essentially rural. The most common source of iron at this period
was bog iron, which, as its name suggests, is often found underneath
bogs. Most ironworking sites outside the Highlands are to be found in
south-west Scotland and are usually visible now as grass-covered
bloomery mounds made up of slag. The iron produced was distributed
to the many rural furnaces documented, or to urban smiths.

To date, only one example of a smelting site has been excavated –
at Millhill, New Abbey, in Kirkudbrightshire – and the dating,
tentatively 1200–1300 on the basis of pottery found nearby, is not
well-established. Excavation revealed a hearth and a stone structure.
The crevices between the stones of this structure were filled with
fused clay with a yellow-green glaze like that on medieval pottery,
indicative of a high temperature and charcoal samples suggest that
hazel and oak were used for firing.

There is evidence for the use of water power in smelting in England
in the late fourteenth century, in the aftermath of the Black Death.
However, to date, there is no trace of water-powered smelting in
Scotland until the seventeenth century. This seems unlikely given the
development of Scottish cannon production in the fifteenth century.

Lead Mining

In the medieval countryside lead was used to roof the better-endowed
churches and manors, for water piping in the monasteries, and also to
line the coffins of the rich. We do not know how far the Scots market
was infiltrated by lead from England, but we do know that Scottish

military campaigns in Northumbria in 1172–73 disrupted the lead industry in the north of England. Until the thirteenth century, for technological reasons, the getting of lead in Scotland, as in England and Wales, was probably tied to the extraction of silver – lead was smelted from silver-rich lead ore, the residue of the silver extraction process.

The exclusive exploitation of lead ore (galena) was conducted by following the outcrop of the ore in trenches or pits, leaving a distinctive linear pattern of pits on the landscape that may be seen in various parts of Scotland, such as at Sillar Holes, Peeblesshire. Recent earthmoving to create a pond uncovered a medieval midden, presumably rubbish dumped into one of the old workings by the lead-miners. This midden was waterlogged and so preserved pieces of cloth and leather as well as rope and wood. Sherds of White Gritty Ware cooking pots found in the midden date it roughly to the twelfth to fourteenth century.

Coal Mining

The documentation of coal exploitation can be confusing because the word 'coal' is also used for charcoal. Until the eighteenth century the extraction of coal was limited to the exploitation of surface outcrops. Mines comprised sloping entrance passage-ways and bell-pit shafts, so-called because of the bell-shaped gallery formed by exploiting the area immediately around the shaft when the seam was reached. Such pits can be identified by the dimpled spoil tip on the surface at the mouth of the shaft. Newbattle Abbey and the local lord were exploiting coal in Tranent parish in Lothian in the thirteenth century, and there are records of mining in the Dolphington area of Lothian in 1526 where vertical shafts were accessed by spiral stairs. Opencast mining in East Lothian has encountered shafts of earlier periods, but surface identification can be difficult. Near Slamannan, Stirlingshire, eighteenth-century pits depicted on plans are no longer visible on the surface and some have been covered by agricultural rig.

The monks of Newbattle Abbey appear to have been most concerned with the exploitation of coal in the Lothians, while the monks of Kelso required their tenants at Redden Grange to carry coal from Berwick to Kelso at the end of the thirteenth century. This coal may have been mined near Berwick since coal is to be found just south of the town, or could have been imported from Tyneside. Furthermore, excavations at Kelso have recovered coal and cinder from medieval layers. This suggests that coal was used for domestic heating in some of the great Abbeys and in their dependent settlements.

White Gritty Ware pottery kiln.
A fourteenth-century three-flued pottery kiln at Colstoun, East Lothian. This is an improvement on the two-flue design, also found at the site. This is the only White Gritty Ware production site to have been found to date.
D. HALL

Epilogue

The medieval countryside in Scotland was created by an agrarian revolution that took place in the twelfth and thirteenth centuries, changing the farming landscape of lowland Scotland into one that was familiar across much of northern Europe: the open 'champagne' country depicted by Slezer at the end of the seventeenth century. It was a land in which town and country were defined for the first time; villages and burghs were built, and agricultural surplus was traded in the fairs and markets of the new burghs. Large hunting reserves on a north European model were established to provide venison for the new feudal nobility, whose castles and manors arose at the centres of their estates. New rural industries were introduced, such as the manufacture of ceramics, and there was widespread use of water-mills to process grain. Rural housing adopted the widespread model of the long-house, typically cruck-framed houses with walls of turf, clay and stone, in which humans and animals lived under one roof.

However, the period was marked by fluctuations. The declining late medieval population led to the splitting of unwieldy villages into smaller units. Some villages were abandoned and there was a return to a more dispersed pattern of small touns. By the sixteenth century, particularly in the border counties, the better-placed tenants invested in fortified houses, aping the tower houses of their social superiors. Farming changed as it became common to create temporary enclosures of the outfield, and towards the end of the medieval period there was a renewed expansion of rural settlement, often situated on outfield sites. The pottery industry declined at the same time and emerged in the sixteenth century as a more technically advanced industry, geared to large-scale production; the introduction of tablewares and green-glazed vessels reflected the social changes that were taking place. Such changes were the precursors of the agricultural improvements of the eighteenth century, and show that the medieval runrig system was capable of adaptation.

How Do I Find Out More?

Sites to visit

Many of these sites are in private ownership and you will require permission to explore them. Those in public ownership are indicated (M). The National Monument Record of Scotland number is given at the end of each entry.

Settlements

NY 033 785 Torthorwald, Dumfriesshire – A cruck-framed cottage near the crest of a ridge on the east side of Lochar Moss. The cottage is single-storeyed, gabled, and roofed with straw thatch. The external walls are of lime-washed rubble bonded in mud mortar and pointed with lime. NY07NW30

NT 513 840 Dirleton, Village and Castle (M), East Lothian – A planned medieval village layout with a rare combination of a 13th-century 'green' village and castle. NT58SW52

NT 641 631 Penshiel Grange, Whittingham, East Lothian – A small group of ruins including a vaulted building and the footings of other buildings belonging to the Melrose Abbey grange of Penshiel. NT66SW11

NT 124 339 Campsie Abbot's House and Chapel, Perthshire – The footings of the manor house of the Abbot of Cupar Angus Abbey and the chapel of St. Adomnan are visible on a promontory above the left bank of the River Tay. NO13SW10.

NO 139 637 & 140 636 Lair, Glenshee, Perthshire – Early medieval 'Pitcarmick-type' houses and other medieval round-ended buildings. NO16SW38, 40, 127

NT 845 268 Colpenhope Grange, Witchcleuch Burn, Roxburghshire – The remains of a medieval grange of Kelso Abbey called Colpenhope, which then lay in England. NT82NW39

NY 485 905 Greenshiels Burn, Newcastleton, Roxburghshire – A medieval farmstead comprising five, much-reduced, turf-walled buildings and an enclosure. Three of the buildings appear to have hollows indicating byre-drains in one end. The settlement was abandoned in the early 17th century. NY49SE17

NT 655 076 Martinlee Sike, Southdean, Roxburghshire – A medieval assart enclosure defined by a bank and external ditch, containing two farmsteads and some rig cultivation. NT60NE20

NT 526 273 Midlem Village, Roxburghshire – A classic planned medieval village, comprising four rows of houses and properties arranged around a green. NT52NW20

NT 631 283 Muirhouselaw, Roxburghshire – A moated manor site, comprising two adjacent ditched enclosures. NT62NW1

NT 644 098 Slack's Tower, Roxburghshire – An excellent example of a fortified farmhouse of the later 16th century, surrounded by several other farm buildings reduced to footings. Fields delimited by earthen banks that display traces of rig can be seen on the slopes around the site. NT60NW3

NT 765 173 Upper Chatto Medieval Village, Roxburghshire – The slight earthworks of a medieval village comprising two rows of house-sites on either side of a street lie in the field to the north-west of the modern farmsteading at Upper Chatto. A small moated site lies on the north of the burn below the village. NT71NE76

NS 6177 9887 Ballingrew, Stirlingshire – A moated manor situated in low marshy ground in Flanders Moss. NS69NW5

Land Use

Hunting

NO 663 781 Kincardine Royal Deer Park, Aberdeenshire – A good example of a 13th-century royal hunting park and deer trap serving the royal castle of Kincardine. Documented from 1266, the earthworks comprise a large enclosure that is open at the south, modern farmland having removed all trace of the enclosing deer dyke on this side, and a bank and internal ditch designed to keep deer within the park. Whether it was hedged or palisaded is not known. An extension of the park pale to the north across the Arnbarrow Burn created a deer trap that is open to the south-east. NO67NE 10.01

NY 495 960 Deer Trap, Moated Site, Chapel and Castle of Hermitage (M), Newcastleton, Roxburghshire – A 13th-century earthwork castle and late medieval tower house, close to a 12th–13th-century moated manor site and a 14th-century chapel. The earthworks include a funnel-shaped hunting trap open to the west on either side of Lady's Sike. NY49NE 3, 4, 5

Rig

NJ 313 124 Lynardoch, Glenernan, Strathdon, Aberdeenshire – Two furlongs of broad rig and several terraces that have developed from ploughing diagonally to the slope at Lynardoch in Glenernan. NJ31SW 104

NJ 570 302 Wardhouse, Aberdeenshire – A well-preserved patch of reverse-S broad rig with expanded rigs and baulks at their lower end. NJ53SE 8

NX 267 938 Auchensoul, Ayrshire – Extensive rig with high profile and narrow width, suggesting the ridges were spade-built, perhaps using a light sod-busting plough to start the process of rig formation rather than a heavy mould-board plough. NX29SE 4

NT 586 523 Gairmoor, Berwickshire – Extensive broad rig, reverse-S on plan, with pronounced baulks visible between the ridges. NT55SE 10

NT 277 722 Prestonfield Golf Course, City of Edinburgh – A well-preserved area of broad rig near the centre of Edinburgh with high-backed ridges and reverse-S shape which typifies well-developed medieval rig. NT27SE 596 (Golf Course)

NT 783 208 Braemoor Knowe, Hownam, Roxburghshire – A surviving block of reverse-S broad rig including terracing caused by strip cultivation at an angle to the slope with later narrower gauge ridges over them. NT72SE 17

NC 7323 0341 Little Rogart, Sutherland – A cleared post-medieval township which includes broad rig cultivation. NC 70SW 106

NX 2445 6969 High Eldrig, Wigtonshire – Narrow curving rig with converging ends and lazy-beds lie around the farmstead, which comprises two parallel buildings NX26NW 13

Managed Ancient Woodland

NS 521 707 Garscadden Policies, City of Glasgow – An example of a wood bank (a bank and external ditch) surrounding coppiced oak stools on three sides. This may be a rare example of an enclosed late medieval wood, although the enclosure dyke has not been dated. NS57SW 97

NS 549 771 Near Mugdock Castle, Dumbartonshire – In mixed deciduous woods there are large coppiced oak stools on the sloping ground between the Castle and the Allander Water, with birch and alder coppice in the wetter parts. Thirteenth-century references to woods and the mapped woods on Blaeu and Roy support the physical evidence of stools 2

metres in diameter for the medieval antiquity of the woods. NS57NW 9

NS 728 537 Cadzow Park, Lanarkshire – The park, which was acquired for hunting by James, Lord Roslin in 1445 and later used as an ornamental park, contains gnarled oaks together with some pollarded oaks and coppice stools of medieval antiquity. Rig in the park is either contemporary or later than the park pale. NS75SW 3

NT 335 685 Dalkeith Park, Lothian – The park, although dating from the mid-17th century, is a good example of managed oak woodland with some pollarded and occasional coppiced oaks. It is maintained chiefly as a recreational park today, and still actively grazed. NT36NW 65

Shielings

NS 686 242 Slackshaw Burn, Ayrshire – A group of 11 shieling-huts on a ridge near the west tributary of the Slackshaw Burn. Excavations in the 1920s revealed the turf or stone footings of small buildings. Late medieval pottery was recovered from the site. NS62SE 6

NT 059 911 to 065 911 Craigluscar Hill, Fife – Three groups of turf shieling huts have been located along the ridge of the hill. NT09SE 2, 10, 11

NY 456 880 West Hesleyside, Newcastleton, Roxburghshire – A small group of rectangular huts defined by grass-covered footings with midden heaps is visible in front of the entrances of some of them. NY48NE 154

Rural Industry

Grain-drying

NJ 351 129 The Doune of Invernochty (M), Aberdeenshire – A fine 12th-century motte with a large hall and stone perimeter on the summit. A large keyhole-shaped corn-drying kiln is cut into the upcast material from the ditch on the south. NJ31SE 1

Mineral Extraction

NY 366 820 Burrian Hill, Dumfriesshire – A bloomery mound, 8 metres across and 0.6 metres high, producing iron slag. NY38SE 12

NT 145 533 Sillar Holes, Peeblesshire – The mining remains at Lead Law include a number of small shallow pits surrounded by a rim of spoil, a group of larger pits and spoil dumps more akin to quarrying, and a narrow, steep-sided channel suggestive of a drift mine or adit. The pits and quarries lie on two main east–west alignments, the northern having a greater density of pits. A pond in the north-west corner of the field has recently been enlarged, and lead slag, sherds of medieval cooking pot and organic material, including woollen cloth, leather shoes and rope, were recovered. NT15SW 32

NS 981 717 Hilderston Hills, West Lothian – A string of pits for mineral extraction, partly cut into broad rig, on the slopes of Cairnpapple Hill. NS97SE 97

NS 989 715 Windywa's Silvermine, Cairnpapple Hill, West Lothian – Pits cut into the slopes of Cairnpapple Hill for the extraction of silver. NS97SE 96

Museum Displays

National Museums of Scotland – The medieval rooms include a display of the Sillar Holes' assemblage, medieval pottery and coinage.

HISTORIC SCOTLAND safeguards Scotland's built heritage, including its archaeology, and promotes its understanding and enjoyment on behalf of the Secretary of State for Scotland. It undertakes a programme of 'rescue archaeology', from which many of the results are published in this book series.

Scotland has a wealth of ancient monuments and historic buildings, ranging from prehistoric tombs and settlements to remains from the Second World War, and HISTORIC SCOTLAND gives legal protection to the most important, guarding them against damaging changes or destruction. HISTORIC SCOTLAND gives grants and advice to the owners and occupiers of these sites and buildings.

HISTORIC SCOTLAND has a membership scheme which allows access to properties in its care, as well as other benefits. For information, contact: 0131 668 8999.

Fortified farmhouse.
Cattle, moveable wealth, being driven into a 16th century farm yard in the border counties. At its centre was a fortified farmhouse, typical of those owned by the bonnet laird of this region.
DAVID SIMON

Further Reading

R A Dodgshon *Land and Society in Early Scotland* Oxford Clarendon Press 1981

A A M Duncan *Scotland: the Making of the Kingdom* Oliver & Boyd, 1978

A Fenton *Scottish Country Life* John Donald 1976

S Foster and T C Smout (eds) *The History of Soils and Field Systems* Scottish Cultural Press 1994

A Grant *Independence and Nationhood: Scotland 1306–1469* Edinburgh University Press 1984

M R McCarthy & C M Brooks *Medieval Pottery in Britain AD 902–1600* Leicester University Press 1988

RCAHMS *South-east Perth: an archaeological landscape* HMSO 1994 – the medieval chapters,

RCAHMS *Eastern Dumfriesshire: an archaeological landscape* HMSO 1997 – the medieval chapters

T C Smout (ed) *Scottish Woodland History* Scottish Cultural Press 1997

Peter Yeoman *Medieval Scotland* Batsford 1995

Acknowledgements

I am very grateful to my wife, Rosemary, without whose encouragement and support this book would never have been written. I also wish to thank Neville Moir for his deft management; the editorial contributions of Gordon Barclay and Jackie Henrie, which turned the draft into a book; to David Simon for his excellent reconstructions of the various medieval scenes that illustrate medieval rural life; to the staff of the Royal Commission on the Ancient and Historical Monuments of Scotland for reproducing many of the site images; and to Derek Hall for his helpful discussions on the relation of town and country. My thanks are also due to the following individuals and organisations for permission to reproduce specific illustrations: the Royal Commission on the Ancient and Historical Monuments of Scotland; the Trustees of the Royal Museums of Scotland; the Keeper of the National Archives of Scotland; the British Library; the Forestry Commission; Perth Museum and Art Gallery; Historic Scotland; Derek Hall; Grith Lerche; Sandy Fenton; John Dent; and Matthew Ritchie.